VIRILIO AND THE
MEDIA

Theory and Media

VIRILIO AND THE MEDIA

JOHN ARMITAGE

polity

First published in 2012 by Polity Press

Polity Press
65 Bridge Street
Cambridge CB2 1UR, UK

Polity Press
350 Main Street
Malden, MA 02148, USA

ISBN-13: 978-0-7456-4228-4
ISBN-13: 978-0-7456-4229-1(pb)

A catalogue record for this book is available from the British Library.

Typeset in 10.75 on 14 pt Janson Text
by Servis Filmsetting Ltd, Stockport, Cheshire
Printed and bound in Great Britain by MPG Books Group Limited,
Bodmin, Cornwall

The publisher has used its best endeavours to ensure that the URLs for
external websites referred to in this book are correct and active at the time
of going to press. However, the publisher has no responsibility for the
websites and can make no guarantee that a site will remain live or that the
content is or will remain appropriate.

Every effort has been made to trace all copyright holders, but if any have
been inadvertently overlooked the publisher will be pleased to include any
necessary credits in any subsequent reprint or edition.

For further information on Polity, visit our website: www.politybooks.com

For Joanne

CONTENTS

ACKNOWLEDGMENTS

I am grateful to several people for their supportive contributions to *Virilio and the Media*: Sean Cubitt, who initially suggested the book; Paul Virilio, who will by now be as astonished as I am that this is the fourth volume that I have produced on his work; Andrea Drugan and Lauren Mulholland, who have been consummate editors, tendering assistance, encouragement, and sensitive guidance during my editorship of *Virilio Now: Current Perspectives in Virilio Studies* and the writing of *Virilio and the Media*; and, finally, my good friends at *Cultural Politics*, above all Ryan Bishop and Douglas Kellner, Mark Featherstone, and the artist Joy Garnett, whose bravura painting adorns the cover of this book. Discussing with me almost daily Virilio's ideas concerning the media and much else besides, such splendid companions not only help one to understand the contradictory nature of the world, but also how to cut loose from long-established responses to it.

INTRODUCTION

Paul Virilio (1932–) is one of the leading media theorists of the twenty-first century. He is well known for his innovative studies of the aesthetics of disappearance, which will establish the chief focal point of *Virilio and the Media* and will be explained in detail shortly. The aesthetics of disappearance is the core of his 1980 book of the same title (Virilio 2009a), which is increasingly debated by media theorists and is widely regarded as an important text for undergraduate and postgraduate programs in the visual arts, cinema and new media, cultural and political geography, and museum studies. It is the primary text of his aesthetic theory and has become progressively more influential since its first edition. In a virtuoso sequence of four concise parts, he examines perception and speed, politics, society, the convulsive state of human consciousness, subjectivity, and absence.

This book will be the topic of Chapter 1. His numerous further media-related writings, composed throughout an extensive intellectual career, also reveal a widespread concern with war, vision, and urban terrorism and provoke stimulating questions for anyone studying the contemporary arts and humanities, social sciences, and philosophy. The aim of *Virilio and the Media* is to familiarize readers with a range of Virilio's decisive critical investigations into today's media world and to clarify his aesthetics and philosophy of disappearance.

Important questions about art and technology, aesthetics, and disappearance are situated at the heart of Virilio's work on the media. And, whether he is writing about a masterpiece of cinema, a military text, logistics, or human perception, he constantly focuses upon the significant artistic and technological concerns that his subject calls to mind. Virilio is, first and foremost, a critic of art and a philosopher of technology involved with how our ways of life are arranged and managed by the cultures we live in, and his examination of everything – from new media and vision to inertia, the mobile phone, and accidents – plays a part in this critical appreciation. His persistent contestation of traditional ideas about the city and about panic, violence, territory, and televised media events makes his work frequently worrying and complex, but simultaneously exhilarating and affecting.

While Virilio does not continually employ his own concept, a great deal of his writing on the media concentrates on questions emerging from what he terms "the aesthetics of disappearance." The idea of an aesthetics of disappearance has attained a somewhat fashionable – if fatalistic – reputation lately. It is regularly associated with the work of the late French media theorist Jean Baudrillard (1929–2007) – for example with a contemporary cultural "world from which human beings have disappeared" and with the dismissal of arguments for their "natural" exhaustion, extinction, or even extermination (2009: 9–10). Commentators on the aesthetics of disappearance who focus on the exhaustion of natural resources or on the extinction of species are often criticized for their conviction that in current media theory the question of the aesthetics of disappearance has to do with physical processes or natural phenomena. Thus the argument that Baudrillard (2009: 10) produces is based on the notion that the human species is "the only one to have invented a specific mode of disappearance that has nothing to do with Nature's law," and that the aim of media theory is merely to explore and take pleasure in an emergent "art of disappearance." Baudrillard's account of the aesthetics of disappearance is very different from Virilio's philosophical perspective. Similarly, Baudrillard's suggestion that, in the era of the aesthetics of disappearance, the human species has been appropriated by the "disappearance of the real" and by "the murder of reality in the age of the media, virtual reality, and networks" is a proposal that Virilio acknowledges but resists throughout his work. For, even if he concedes that the human species has created forms of disappearance beyond the laws of nature, his writings on the media continuously take up the issue of what it might mean to theorize and act ethically without the existence of the human species, its art, or even reality itself. Virilio does not simply recoil in misery at humanity's decision to transform the real world in the modern age through technoscience; nor does he rejoice at the defeat of pre-technoscientific analysis or knowledge, notwithstanding the relentless implementation of technoscientific inventions. Instead he steadfastly looks for novel ways of examining the aesthetic realms of technoscientific devices and their cultures in order to determine alternative trajectories for media theory and practice, which will transform these and our own worlds into something more human and caring. Hence, for Virilio, the most important work of a philosopher of aesthetics is to challenge, with equal force, both the sliding of human beings into a phase of technologically induced disappearance and the overwhelming strength of those modes of disappearance that lie outside of Nature's law. These are all difficult conceptions, but each and every one will be presented straightforwardly and in depth in subsequent chapters.

Due to the questions raised in his writings on the media, Virilio has exercised a strong influence all throughout the arts and humanities, social sciences, and philosophy. For the undergraduate reading cinema or new media studies, Virilio's theory offers a variety of ways in which one could interrogate conventional media processes, businesses, methods, and our opinions about culture. Crucial ideas about cinema, for instance the warfare-derived "logistics of perception" and "the vision machine," which are described in Chapters 2 and 3 respectively, engender persuasive approaches toward reimagining the culture and politics of film; and his assertions concerning the damaging results of digital, computerized, or networked information and communication technologies make his media theory of "polar inertia" and of numerous other catastrophes wholly applicable to contemporary global media studies. The postgraduate cultural or political geographer can discover in Virilio's work on the media stimulating investigations and new understandings of the writings of several leading ancient and modern philosophers concerned with the city: above all, Aristotle (384–322 BC) and Martin Heidegger (1889–1976), on top of more current thinkers like the French philosopher Maurice Merleau-Ponty (1908–61), the philosopher and film theorist Gilles Deleuze (1925–95), with whom Virilio co-invented numerous concepts, such as "control societies" (Virilio and Armitage 2011: 30), and well-known postmodern media theorists such as Baudrillard. Virilio's extensive awareness of the modern city and its culture of panic, which is introduced in Chapter 4, over and above his theorization of their philosophical, political, and geographical significance, is of particular importance to those researching in television, media, and the cultural studies of contemporary events. Furthermore, while Virilio does not frequently write about individual artworks, his critical studies of art, technology, and the "Museum of Accidents," which are discussed in Chapter 5, make him a vital philosopher for anyone with a concern for contemporary aesthetics and media theory and with a critical approach to contemporary art and technology. On every single one of these subjects, Virilio offers a distinctive intellectual perspective, a variety of compelling critical concepts concerning aesthetics, a call for honesty about the nature of technology, and the courage to ignore disciplinary boundaries.

VIRILIO'S INTELLECTUAL BIOGRAPHY

In *Pure War* (2008) Virilio sketches his position as a media theorist (or, as he describes himself, as a "critic of the art of technology") in down-to-earth language:

> When someone says to me, "I don't understand your position," my response is, "I'll explain it to you: I am a critic of the art of technology." Fair enough? That's all. If they still don't understand, then I say: "Just look at what an art critic is to traditional art, and then substitute technology for traditional art, and you have my position." It's that simple. (Virilio and Lotringer 2008: 192)

Elsewhere Virilio has disclosed that, as a "war baby," he has "been deeply marked by the accident, the catastrophe, and thus by sudden changes, and upheavals" and that he attended the lectures at the Sorbonne of the philosophers Maurice Merleau-Ponty, Jean Wahl, and Vladimir Jankelevitch (Virilio and Armitage 2001: 16–18). Virilio was born in

Paris in 1932. However, his ultimate vocation as a French media theorist began after his involvement in city planning, in problems regarding the militarization of the cultural, and in the control of terrain after his encounters with Nazi-occupied France during World War II – encounters that also deeply influenced his writings. In 1958 he commenced long-term research into the "Atlantic Wall" – that is, the 15,000 Nazi military bunkers built during World War II, the length of the shoreline of France, to resist any Allied seaborne offensive. To some extent he was trying to understand, transform, and implement the later thought of the famed Swiss architect Le Corbusier (1887–1966). To encapsulate Le Corbusier's arguments succinctly, his architectural view-point during the 1940s and 1950s supported the rejection of his previously rational flat glass and metal designs, which up to that point Le Corbusier had been active in promoting, and made for a shift toward a new, anti-rational and aggres-sively sculptural style, which was eventually to prove equally influential. Hence, according to Le Corbusier, the mission of the modern architect was to construct buildings like his Unité d'Habitation at Marseille (1947–52), with its weighty bare concrete appendages and eccentric roof. Throughout his period as a researcher Virilio wrote many contentious articles concerning the condition of architecture in France and became engaged with the trajectories of urban plan-ning, which slowly developed into a complete media theory, focused on perception and a cultural philosophy of military history.

By 1963, together with the architect Claude Parent, Virilio had established Architecture Principe, which was a post-Le Corbusier architectural grouping with an eponymous jour-nal, *Architecture Principe*. The two set in motion their own architectural theory of "the function of the oblique," which gave rise to the building of two important structures: the

Church of Saint-Bernadette du Banlay at Nevers (1966)
and the Thomson-Houston Center of Aerospace Research
in Vélizy-Villacoublay (1969) (see Virilio and Parent 1996a,
1996b). Based in Paris, Virilio embarked on publishing many
articles directed at revising and radicalizing Le Corbusier's
ideas for modern architecture. He also participated, enthu-
siastically, in the general strike and student-led occupation
protests of May 1968. In 1969 he was designated professor
and workshop director at the École Spéciale d'Architecture in
Montparnasse and, partially as a result of the "events" of May
1968, he began to investigate the associations between architecture, space, the city, and the military. This investigation
brought about the publication of *Bunker Archeology* (1994a),
possibly even today his most multifaceted and groundbreaking book, which grew out of his 1975 "Bunker Archeology"
photography exhibition at the Museum of Decorative Arts in
Paris. This volume of short essays and photographs is exciting and frequently extremely worrying. *Bunker Archeology*
opens with a thorough account of how military space can
be exposed and expanded so as to form an architectural and
political cartography or chronology of war landscapes. It
continues through an examination of the architecture of the
military bunker, and it ends with a Le Corbusier-inflected
analysis of the temporal and spatial transformations shaped
by conflict and by the advent of the "Atlantic Wall." I do not
discuss *Bunker Archeology* in this book. But what is important
to note here is that, through its probing of military space
such as the Le Corbusier-like monolithic fortress of the military bunker, this book prefigures Virilio's later writings on
the aesthetics of disappearance by means of a text-free series
of photographs entitled "An Aesthetics of Disappearance"
(1994a: 167–80).

Virilio's later work on the aesthetics of disappearance was
preceded by his writings of the 1970s, for example *L'Insécurité*

du territoire (1976), *Speed and Politics: An Essay on Dromology* (2006), and *Popular Defense and Ecological Struggles* (1990), in addition to a succession of significant articles on contemporary geopolitics and the military, transportation, and warfare. These texts are not, however, the keystone of his aesthetics of disappearance or media theory. Consequently, it is Virilio's *The Aesthetics of Disappearance* that will be the focal point of *Virilio and the Media* and shape its development. For, with the publication of *The Aesthetics of Disappearance* and its translation into various languages, Virilio became a leading media theorist, whose writings now influence other media theorists and critics worldwide.

For this reason, all of Virilio's subsequent media-related works enlarge on *The Aesthetics of Disappearance* to some degree and advance novel approaches to the consideration of contemporary conflict, film, and the city. One of his most powerful media-inflected texts is *War and Cinema: The Logistics of Perception* (1989), which contains several of his key and insightful articles composed following *The Aesthetics of Disappearance*. This and other texts (e.g. Virilio 1991, 1994b, 1995, 1997, 2000a, 2000b, 2000c, 2000d, 2002a, 2002b) will be referred to throughout the present study to clarify the important concepts and methods presented in his work on the aesthetics of disappearance. Such texts frequently develop hypotheses explained in previous writings, while connecting with different or new questions that Virilio ascertains as confronting media cultures.

Virilio's later media writings are centered on art and accidents, acceleration, the city, ecology, and the university. He habitually revises notions introduced in his previous texts, and he does so in order to produce at times astonishing reinterpretations of major modern and ancient artists and authors, for instance the twentieth-century Italian artist/poet Filippo Tommaso Emilio Marinetti (1876–1944) and the

British science fiction novelist H. G. Wells (1866–1946) in *Art and Fear* (2003a) and *Unknown Quantity* (2003b), or the ancient Chinese military philosopher Sun Tzu (*c.* sixth century BC) in the 1985 text *Negative Horizon*, which remained untranslated until 2005 (2005a). These sometimes difficult works, along with *City of Panic* (2005b), *The Original Accident* (2007a), *Art As Far As the Eye Can See* (2007b), *Grey Ecology* (2009b), and *The University of Disaster* (2010a) are all instances of his aesthetic thinking in operation. Thus they act as outstanding expressions of what is at issue in Virilio's wider philosophical conceptualization of critique, art, technology, and the Museum of Accidents in particular (which will be explained in Chapter 5).

Virilio's most recent writings on the media, for example *The Futurism of the Instant: Stop-Eject* (2010b) and *The Great Accelerator* (2012), are formed by an impatient frustration with the conventional understandings of contemporary human dislocation and history and by an awareness of the significance of conflicts and other disasters that bring widespread anxiety. He ceaselessly interrogates established media theory and its futures, and he is always prepared to revise his own previous conjectures on today's instantaneous media, where privacy is increasingly a thing of the past. For Virilio, both media theory and media practice should frequently be amended by examining, for instance, the future of the human community and its relocation through the development of the city of panic and by contemplating their worth and purpose in the context of present-day cultural acceleration and exodus from the modern city; and, if they are revealed to be deficient, then they have to be changed to embrace, for example, the estimated "645 million people" who "will be displaced from their homes over the next forty years because of large-scale development projects like intensive mining or the building of hydroelectric dams" (Virilio 2010b: 1). "Virilian" media theory, therefore, is not a "grand theory" of the media but a modest collection of tools that can be used to illuminate various and diverse urban and historical events – and much more besides. Thus, for Virilio, his "critique of the art of technology" seeks, among other things, to respond to the distinctiveness of the contemporary exodus, and it repeatedly struggles to re-create itself in view of the latest media events – such as the present formation of a global city of flows or the disturbing prospect of the whole of humanity being on the move. Resembling the "hypermodern" (Armitage 2000, 2011) philosophers, *cinéastes*, and military, new media, urban, and art theorists with whom he spends his days, Virilio unlocks novel theoretical viewpoints on the media, which have the capability to reconceptualize our increasingly transitory, estranged, and exiled planet Earth and to turn it into something superior to this contemporary world of insanity that is unregulated technoscience. Moreover, it is this receptiveness to "Plan B" that makes Virilio's writings on the media so interesting, demanding, and encouraging.

FIVE KEY CONCEPTS: AESTHETICS AND BEYOND

Five concepts will be the key factors in the consideration of Virilio's writings on the media in this book: "aesthetics" and "cinema," "new media," "city," and "museum." Ever since *The Aesthetics of Disappearance*, the connections linking these ideas, together with the possibilities they present for philosophy, film, new media, urban, and museum studies, have been very important for Virilio. None of these concepts is simple to explain. What is more, each one of them has been argued over by media and cultural theorists. The objective of the present book is to render Virilio's examination of these key concepts as transparent and comprehensible as is practicable.

Even so, prior to deliberating in depth on his particular deployment of them, I want to summarize how they are presently used by other media and cultural theorists. Besides offering an approximate definition of the concepts, this will also establish the background to contemporary discussions concerning aesthetics and so on. What, for example, is the relationship between aesthetics and cinema? Does the arrival of cinema entail a revision of traditional aesthetics? Does cinema substitute aesthetics? Or disturb it? As we shall discover in subsequent chapters, these are questions that Virilio addresses. Consequently it is imperative to consider the links between aesthetics and cinema, new media, the city, and the museum – not least because, for many media and cultural theorists, these concepts indicate diverse ideas. What, then, are media and cultural theorists referring to when they use the concept of "aesthetics'?

Aesthetics

Aesthetics is not usually associated with the subject matter of works of art but with their arrangement or their organizational features, with a consistent "philosophy of art," or with the creative aspects of an entire culture. From the eighteenth century onwards, philosophers such as Immanuel Kant (1724–1804) involved themselves with the nature of the world, with human perception, and with the appraisal of beauty in order to determine the inspiring and eternal characteristics of these subject matters – their deeper intention being to distinguish between what is and what is not art. More recently, Marxist cultural theorists like Terry Eagleton (1990) have argued that Kant actually sought a definition of art that was rooted in its "essence" or ultimate reality and in its "transcendental" or intuitive and spiritual qualities. For Eagleton, Kant's work helped to support capitalist conceptions of individuality and liberty, independence, and cosmopolitanism, conceptions that allied Kant's aesthetics with the leading values and beliefs of modern class-based culture. Aesthetics and art, for Eagleton, are consequently ideologically, culturally, and historically determined and located discourses – a picture that leaves them more undefined in their political nature than that offered by Kant. In the visual arts, a series of diverse movements – from the "modernist" European avant-garde of Dada in the aftermath of World War I to the "postmodernist" American "anti-aesthetics" of Cindy Sherman and Barbara Kruger from the 1980s onwards – disputed recognized ideological and cultural, historical, political, and technological principles concerning what the perceptual realm of aesthetics, or of contemporary artworks, might or must be (Foster 1994). Thus, whereas modernist aesthetics can be described as a late nineteenth- and early twentieth-century style or movement in the arts that deviated considerably from traditional forms of realist representation, postmodernist aesthetics can be defined as a late twentieth-century style or conception in the arts, architecture, and cultural criticism (Jameson 1991; Nicholls 1995). Postmodernist aesthetics therefore marks a departure from modernist aesthetics and is typified by the self-assured deployment of previous styles and conventions, a combination of different creative designs and media technologies, and a mistrust of "grand theories" (Lyotard 1984). However, notwithstanding the disparities between particular philosophers, media and cultural theorists, and art movements, the general motivating force of aesthetics has often been related to debates over ideas such as artistic genius, taste, or judgment – although today the very possibility of a postmodernist aesthetics is frequently questioned on the grounds of the seemingly increasing rupture between the arts, morality, and politics.

Cinema

Cinema is often linked with contemporary media and cultural theorists writing after the postmodernist aesthetics of the 1980s, following the emergence of postmodern texts that have now become archetypal, such as Fredric Jameson's *Postmodernism, Or, The Cultural Logic of Late Capitalism* (1991) or Ridley Scott's 1981 science fiction film *Blade Runner*. Some postmodern media and cultural theorists portray the logic of contemporary cinematic images not in terms of traditional aesthetics or as conventional forms of perception, but as having an "evil" relationship with their "referent" (the object or idea to which the film or image refers), which is normally presumed to be "reality." They depict cinema as a collection of mediated and technologically transcendent images and invoke the perversity of the correlation between the cinematic image and its referent, "reality." Yet these theorists do so in a manner that implies the permanent bewilderment of cinema goers within the aesthetic field of cinematic images and within the realm of a "reality" whose character people are increasingly unable to understand. There are countless forms of this cinematic fascination, image confusion, and dreamlike states that, for many people, are extremely seductive. Baudrillard (2000), for instance, argues that it is the referent of the image, the supposed "real world" and its "real" objects, that has to be disbelieved, since in cinema it is simply not true that images refer to, or reproduce, things that either rationally or sequentially occur before they do in the "real world" or in "real time." As simulated representations, cinematic images come before "reality" and thus overturn its fundamental and rational order through reproduction. Indeed, according to Baudrillard, film-makers such as Woody Allen represent people as identical and contemporary media culture as the culture of endless reproduction, while simultaneously raising new questions. A good example of Baudrillard's discussion of an Allen film is *Zelig*, produced in 1983, where Allen represents the character Zelig as attempting to develop his own difference and individuality. But, for Baudrillard, Zelig merely finds himself looking like everybody else. In asking questions about individual uniqueness and the seduction of the Other, *Zelig* therefore knowingly uses various cinematic styles and complex strategies to shape an image of widespread contemporary psychological conformity.

Accordingly, cinema's postmodernist aesthetics can be seen as a reaction against the principles and practices of a modernist aesthetics where people start to look like each other and like all that surrounds them. For several feminist media and cultural theorists, such as Grace (2008), Baudrillard's concentration on sameness and seduction is, however, a major problem – mostly because of feminism's commitment to distancing itself from the stereotypical figure of the seductive female. Nevertheless, for Baudrillard, seduction disturbs recognized ideas of similarity and the Other, individualism and compliance, and this permits it to maintain a significant critical function.

New media

Generally, to consider media from a theoretical standpoint is to contemplate the communication channels through which news and entertainment, speech, education, information, and the promotional messages of advertising, together with the beliefs that lie beneath them, are distributed. Yet the recent merger of mediated means of communication with digital technologies and computers – or with "new media" such as desktop and online publishing tools, digital television, mobile phones, computer games, the Internet, and graphics editing programs like Adobe Photoshop – is a challenge to the more modern forms of cultural institution, such as cinema or television. In postmodern culture, political and media philosophers and sociologists frequently claim, cinema's and television's modern methods of organizing vision, technology, and the realms of human stasis and movement have to be reevaluated, because they are increasingly obsolete. The French political and media philosophers Gilles Deleuze and Bernard Stiegler, for example, argue that in what Deleuze calls "control societies" the current, ultrarapid introduction of new media into the democratic process obliterates modern "disciplinary" societies and "time-delayed" modes of political and sociocultural organization (Deleuze 1995; Stiegler 2010). Both for Deleuze and for Stiegler, then, these newly developed forms of control and techniques of mediated production entail a shift from 1980s' media, print, and analog cinematic and broadcast logics and models to previously separate but now convergent new media production systems, which involve video, DVD, and computer-generated imaging as well as the digitally technologized and mediated practices and principles used in their application as representational machines. Such changes clearly indicate that the aesthetic methods of examining the "mechanical reproduction" of "old media" – for instance of newspapers, magazines, books, and cinema – developed by twentieth-century philosophers like Walter Benjamin (1968) have to be reconsidered. Equally, for the Spanish urban sociologist Manuel Castells, these same productive means of convergent new media render most modern forms of media analysis outdated in the era of "the rise of the network society" (2000). The growth of new media indicates therefore that issues concerning the production of images, the distribution of information, and the consumption of mediated communication have to be addressed in new ways as old media is restructured. Indeed, the question is whether such problems can be confronted at all in the face of a new media that not only entails a groundbreaking means of "communication power," but also new ways of considering and doing things with digitized visual representations and with the technologized sensations that electronic devices such as mobile phones produce (Castells 2009).

City

The concept of the "city" is employed to signify something very different from that of "new media." If new media is a postmodern technological development, nineteenth- and twentieth-century cities in particular are generally understood as important manifestations of "modernity," typically defined by processes of increased economic efficiency, sociopolitical calculation, and the rational administration of cultural life. Such processes shaped technological and scientific development or "modernization," while new types of transportation (the railway, the car, the airplane), new means of communication (radar, radio broadcasting, television), and scientific inventions (air conditioning, neon lights, frozen food) aided the unparalleled movement and build-up of newly urbanized populations. The modern city is therefore a much broader concept than new media, and it tries to evoke, for example, the state of mind of urban inhabitants lost in the obscurity of the metropolitan masses (Simmel 1969; Williams 1973). Additionally, the historical era associated with the modern city is brief when compared to the discussions of Kantian aesthetics that began in the eighteenth century, although the birth of the modern city does coincide with the invention of cinema in the late nineteenth century. Sociologists, cultural geographers, and urban theorists have argued over where to situate the sociocultural, literary, and artistic beginnings and expansion of the modern city. For most, the modern city starts with the industrial upheaval of European and American rural sociocultural life in the nineteenth century. There social and cultural critics observed the spread of urban capitalist society, the expansion of the railway and of metropolitan areas, and the early stages of the obliteration of rustic attitudes and existence – which, amid other important developments, led in the 1920s and 1930s to the famous studies of new urban lifestyles conducted by the Chicago School sociologist Louise Wirth (Le Gates and Stout 1996).

However, for many contemporary sociologists, the epoch straddling the close of the twentieth century and the opening of the twenty-first is the epoch in which the modern city gave way to the "postmodern city." Kevin A. Lynch's (1960) conception of "mental maps," together with Richard Sennett's (2003) ideas about the revolution occurring in urban planning and architectural design, for instance, have both been important to the ongoing theorization of the cultural and historical phase of "postmodernity" exemplified by global capitalism or by the highly developed and visibly sign-laden, consumer-driven network societies and urban surroundings of 21st-century Europe, the United States, and Australasia.

What these theories of the modern and the postmodern city share is that they understand such cities as junctures where we begin to re-imagine ourselves and our urban environment. Above all, we are currently imagining ourselves and our metropolitan environs with regard to postmodern architectural transformation, to the historic demolition, in major cities, of scores of modernist "international-style" urban projects, often influenced by Le Corbusier (Jencks 2007). As maintained by the British cultural geographer David Harvey (1991), the idea of the postmodern city articulates the belief that the future of the modern city, of "the condition of postmodernity," has already commenced. For the postmodern city is no longer a modern city but a seemingly ahistorical, and perhaps monotonous, futuristic city based on the ever expanding novelties of consumer culture and on computerized or televisual imagery and media events, in addition to technologies such as mobile phones and iPads. Altered histories, socio-economic arrangements, political and cultural forms of organization, as well as the relentless intensity of "time–space compression" and of new ideas concerning the urban landscape, employment relationships, and the fundamental laws of capital accumulation involving the continuously unequal amassing and distribution of wealth complete Harvey's multidisciplinary conception of the postmodern city. In short, the postmodern city is often viewed as a scene of leisure and tourism that entails the contemporary growth of Western notions of urbanization, sensations of decenteredness, enormity, multiculturalism, and the shift towards increasingly diverse and computer-designed buildings, amusingly ornamented with natural forms. The postmodern city is thus a city in a stylistic condition of permanent fluctuation. The expansion of Las Vegas and Los Angeles, for example, changes the nature of inner-city representations and of visual and linguistic discourses, while furthering ideas about knowledge, technology, "decentered" personal identities, feelings, individualization, and neighborhoods, all of which find themselves bafflingly (dis)"located" within contemporary urban consumer culture (Lyon 1999). Postmodern cities, then, produce disjointed cultural thoughts, questions, and answers among their scattered and ever more numerous inhabitants. However, it is also here that the dissimilarities between different peoples and their consumer choices become the foundation of economic urban systems and postmodern or "global" cities like

London, New York, and Tokyo, all of which are key inter-
sections for today's worldwide monetary network (Sassen
2001). Virilio's examination of postmodern cities is described
in Chapter 4.

Museum

The contemporary art museum is a place of memory, of
inspiration for studying the arts, and, increasingly, mass and
new media technologies such as television and cinema, photography, video, DVDs, digital computing, and the Internet
(see Carbonell 2003; Rush 2005; and Macdonald 2010). The
twenty-first century art museum is therefore a postmodern
museum. It is a particular location for the storage and conservation, categorization, and public display of precious objects,
from ancient drawings to video games. For instance, the
Guggenheim Museum Bilbao in Spain opened as a postmodern "public" museum of visual art in 1997. However, its and
other contemporary museums' conception of the "public" is
complicated by the fact that certain exhibitions necessitate
entrance fees, although the term "public" does distinguish
museums from elite private salons, where artworks are shown
to 'by invitation only' visitors (Harris 2006; Barrett 2010).
The postmodern art museum is important because its survival indicates the sustained recognition of an aesthetic value
and critical theoretical rationale for the work of art that are
no longer dependent upon the premeditated and methodical
efforts of the state – be it premodern religious or modern
– to form people's perceptions, cognitions, and behavior in
order to attain reactions that advanced its preferred inten-
tions and that had been characteristic of European art since
the fourteenth century (Boswell and Evans 1999). In addition, the contemporary art museum involves the production
of art experts. Curators, for example, choose and look after

the museum's artworks; exhibition organizers position and explain the import of artworks when the latter are publicly presented; and, lastly, art critics write and publish knowledgeable assessments of contemporary artworks typically derived from their experience of attending art exhibitions at museums.

These national and increasingly global postmodern art museums are also significant because they frequently symbolize their patrons' lofty beliefs (Henry Tate, Solomon R. Guggenheim, and the like) or represent the aims of the state (nationalism, progress, and so on). Yet the operations of the contemporary art museum are equally powerful regarding the introduction of novel techniques of storage, the improvement of conservation practices, and the corporate or state-sponsored exercise in advertising or international relations that is the blockbuster touring exhibition.

The concepts of "museum" and "gallery" appear to be identical in the visual arts, as both amass, preserve, categorize, and show historically produced *objets d'art* from around the globe. Nonetheless, in the twentieth century, organizations were set up to gather and exhibit specifically modern art – which had the seemingly obvious, yet actually complex result of distinguishing the "museum" from the "gallery." The "museum," for instance, is more and more understood as an organization that cares for items from the past, while the "gallery" is appreciated as an institution that looks after contemporary works of art. But the existence of Spain's Guggenheim Museum Bilbao of contemporary art and the presence of European art from the thirteenth century onwards in the United Kingdom's National Gallery in London pose problems for such conceptions. Even so, these organizations are immensely powerful, because they are integral to the monetary and aesthetic valuation of artworks, to art education, and to related ideas concerning nationality and civilization, the public, the economy, and government. The Guggenheim Museum Bilbao, for example, partly due to its postmodern or "deconstructive" titanium design by Canadian American architect Frank Gehry, is a significant emblem of Spanish culture and present-day Bilbao metropolitan life in the Basque Country. Over 10 million people have visited this arbitrarily curled, radically carved, public museum of art, even if some suggest that it is the naturally contoured building itself rather than the art inside it that draws people to it (Witcomb 2003).

Virilio's reflections on aesthetics and cinema, new media, the city, and the museum incorporate many of the concepts explained above. However, his investigations from *The Aesthetics of Disappearance* to *The Great Accelerator* question almost every one of the media and other theorists thus far mentioned. In the following chapters of this book the specific character of Virilio's explorations of the aesthetics of disappearance will be presented.

CONCLUSION: *VIRILIO AND THE MEDIA*

Virilio and the Media adopts a broadly (but not exclusively) chronological perspective on Virilio's writings on the media because most readers initially encounter his media theory through *The Aesthetics of Disappearance*. Accordingly, this book begins with a comprehensive interpretation of this text, so as to specify clearly what is in the balance in its argument concerning the aesthetics of disappearance. The following chapters reveal numerous subjects produced by this examination, while thoroughly investigating Virilio's claims regarding how we can react – philosophically and methodologically, technologically, and visually – to the aesthetics of disappearance. Chapter 2 scrutinizes a vital concept in Virilio's writings on the media – the logistics of perception – by means of a careful analysis of his significant treatise on twentieth-century movies and conflict, *War and Cinema: The Logistics of Perception*, and it demonstrates how Virilio connects cinematic ideas of war to the aesthetics of disappearance. Since his media theory is particularly attentive to understanding the implications of vision and related technologies such as the mobile phone, Chapter 3 evaluates Virilio's important arguments on these topics by introducing *The Vision Machine* (1994b), *Polar Inertia* (2000a), and *The University of Disaster* (2010a). Chapter 4 inquires into the topic of the city in the age of panic and considers Virilio's reactions to terrorism and televised media events. Chapter 5 revisits art and deliberates on Virilio's critical appreciation of technology and culture, in addition to relating his views on aesthetic critique, the Museum of Accidents, and the fate of the contemporary art museum. This last substantial chapter thus probes into Virilio's thoughts on contemporary art and technology and examines his beliefs about what the work of the aesthetic critic and that of the critic of the art of technology should be. While *Virilio and the Media* slowly develops an image of Virilio's writings on the media, readers can skip to individual chapters if a topic is of particular relevance to their studies. Chapter 5 is followed by a brief concluding chapter, which discusses how other media theorists are adopting and adapting Virilio's conceptions, and it weighs up the influence of his writings on media theory. The book closes with a Guide to Further Reading, a non-technical Glossary of Virilio's key media concepts, and a set of References containing his main writings and the other texts used in the research for this book.

Virilio and the Media is not a stand-in for reading Virilio's own texts on the media. Instead, its goal is to allow readers to set about those texts with greater self-assurance and knowledge, an extremely valuable exercise in and of itself. Reading Virilio is always exciting, and it is hard to overestimate the significance of his media theory for appreciating critically the art and technologies of our contemporary world.

1

THE AESTHETICS OF
DISAPPEARANCE

INTRODUCTION

Media theorists generally associate Paul Virilio with his conception of the "aesthetics of disappearance." This chapter examines his contribution to the debates over contemporary aesthetics by considering one of his most powerful texts, *The Aesthetics of Disappearance* (2009a). It explains the importance of the argument of this book in order to afford an entry point into it for uninitiated English-speaking readers. The chapter then surveys the ramifications of Virilio's study for theorizing and practicing media in the present period.

The theme of the book is the development and modern-day condition of human perception in the world's advanced cultures. Virilio's text is therefore about how diverse ways of perceiving and coping with the realms of photography and technology, science, and cinema are appreciated and incorporated into postmodern culture.

The Aesthetics of Disappearance has gradually become one of

Virilio's most extensively read, culturally important, influential, and contentious books. Originally published in French in 1980, it has attracted comments from theorists in various subjects. Indeed, *The Aesthetics of Disappearance* has not only provided the setting for many contemporary explanations of the aesthetics of disappearance, but also provoked critical debates, arguments, and questions that are influencing the way in which subjects like cultural politics and philosophy carry out their research (Cubitt 2011: 68–91).

Arguably the principal claim of the text is its definition of the aesthetics of disappearance as an "irresistible project and projection toward a technical beyond" (Virilio 2009a: 103). Before presenting a definition as to what Virilio means when he employs concepts such as "aesthetics" or the "technical beyond," it is vital to grasp how this assertion stems from *The Aesthetics of Disappearance* in its entirety. Consequently, the purpose of this chapter is to offer a foundation for an appreciation of what Virilio means by defining the aesthetics of disappearance in this way.

THE WORLD AS WE SEE IT IS PASSING: AN AESTHETIC APPROACH TO THE WORLD OF "PICNOLEPSY"

The most productive location for starting to uncover what *The Aesthetics of Disappearance* is about is its epigraph, "*The world as we see it is passing.* Paul of Tarsus" (Virilio 2009a: 17), which instantly offers vital signs about its form and subject matter.

Primarily the book can be portrayed as an aesthetic approach to the world. Typically, as we saw in the Introduction, the concepts "aesthetic" and "aesthetics" have both a restricted and an extended usage, and they can be employed to identify the formal or organizational facets of artworks in contrast to their apparent topics. *The Aesthetics of Disappearance*'s standing as an aesthetic creation is obvious from the way Virilio struggles to present it as a consistent philosophy of art, as a commentary on the artistic aspects of contemporary culture as a whole. His aesthetics, then, welcomes the examination of all of these subjects and objects. Put differently, *The Aesthetics of Disappearance* offers an explanation of the character of seeing, of our awareness and beliefs about it, and of its passage into disappearance. Its goal is to unearth fundamental tendencies and associations between different concepts and sensations and to outline as unambiguously as possible the growth of an aesthetics of disappearance in postmodern philosophy and culture.

Another important concept on the opening page is "picnolepsy," which he describes and defines as follows (p. 19):

> The lapse occurs frequently at breakfast and the cup dropped and overturned on the table is its well-known consequence. The absence lasts a few seconds; its beginning and its end are sudden. The senses function, but are nevertheless closed to external impressions. The return being just as sudden as the departure, the arrested word and action are picked up again where they have been interrupted. Conscious time comes together again automatically, forming a continuous time without apparent breaks. For these absences, which can be quite numerous, hundreds every day most often pass completely unnoticed by others around – we'll be using the word "picnolepsy" (from the Greek *picnos* [*sic*]: frequent). However, for the picnoleptic, nothing really has happened, the missing time never existed. At each crisis, without realizing it, a little of his or her life simply escaped.

Virilio maintains that he is examining the state of picnolepsy throughout the historical development of human cultures. But what does he mean? The notion, for instance, of an aesthetic approach to the world of the awe-inspiring and eternal features of beauty, or of an approach to discriminating against what is dependent and thus not "art," is comparatively simple. Both approaches rely on clues that can be observed if we want to verify our deductions: the aesthetic "genius" of Michelangelo's statue of David, perhaps, or "taste" as the everyday manifestation of personal opinion across the popular arts, entertainment, fashion, and daily life. But what does it mean to adopt an aesthetic approach to the world, or to the state of picnolepsy? Obviously, this state is not a clear-cut case of chronic lack of visual sensation and functioning: *The Aesthetics of Disappearance* is not merely a catalog of the newer developments in human awareness, appearance, and visual disruption. What is in the balance is a great deal more significant.

The focal point for Virilio is the character and condition of picnolepsy. What is picnolepsy? How has it been produced, arranged, and used over the centuries in human cultures? *The Aesthetics of Disappearance* is thus a book about how ancient, modern, and postmodern human cultures behave toward perceptual stability and breaks, photography, technology, consciousness, and time. Virilio explores which kinds of picnolepsy function automatically and which we assimilate. He asks how picnolepsy is conveyed as uninterrupted time, devoid of perceptible interruptions, and who has access to these numerous everyday absences, which frequently occur while being totally ignored by others around us. What are they used for? Who decides on and manages the direction of picnolepsy? How does it form the "picnoleptic," her existence or his encounters with the absent time of the world?

The key question of *The Aesthetics of Disappearance* as a book about "the world as we see it" and its "passing" is therefore: How are human existence and individuality created through historically conditioned configurations of picnolepsy? This is an important question for Virilio, because the condition of picnolepsy is such that, without being conscious of it, fractions of our lives are evading us, particularly as the advanced cultures some time ago crossed the threshold of the postindustrial and postmodern age of the aesthetics of disappearance. The chief premise and consequently the goal of Virilio's book are to examine accurately the condition of picnolepsy and to explain its aesthetic repercussions.

THE AESTHETICS OF PICNOLEPSY

From the outset, Virilio contends that the improvements in photography and cinema that have occurred since the nineteenth century have influenced not only how picnolepsy is communicated, but also the condition of picnolepsy itself. It is not merely that we can catch more light in cameras and create technological instruments such as darkrooms, lenses, and, nowadays, digital imagery. It is also that these changes in entrapment, photography, and cinema are altering how we employ and assimilate picnolepsy. For the integration of our own bodies with the camera has by now changed the way vision is obtained, categorized, accessed, and used. Consequently, within what Virilio calls the aesthetics of disappearance, picnolepsy itself has altered.

Virilio shows that picnolepsy has become a series of technical prostheses, which are non-natural supplements or substitutes for our continually maturing yet ultimately waning eyes, and which is also increasingly the foundation of art in contemporary culture. Picnolepsy in the form of the light projected by technical prostheses is thus crucial to the production of postmodern artistic perception or aesthetic representations. Certainly, the severance of the two furthest extremities – of the visible and the invisible – of the picnoleptic occurrence, resembling an epileptic seizure unseen and unidentified by almost everybody, is, according to Virilio, already an important mass experience. This is because, for Virilio, in the global realm of contemporary art and aesthetics, picnolepsy has become a kind of waking dream or semiconscious existence, which he calls "*a state of paradoxical waking* (rapid waking)" (2009a: 24–5). The most cinematic of technologies are those that have the maximum picnoleptic means: those with the best technologies of disappearance, the most advanced photography, the most highly developed special effects, and the cinematically accelerated wherewithal to distribute the most intense light to those in a state of paradoxical waking. The worldwide state of paradoxical waking is today dominated by aesthetic questions of picnolepsy and disappearance, just as ancient cultures used to be dominated by aesthetic questions of duration and appearance. Virilio prophesies an era when the images of vision technologies will usurp human-centered picnolepsy, just as photography and the "cinematographic motor" have commandeered the wood, canvas, and marble, which were associated with the paintings and sculptures of former times (p. 25; see also Virilio and Armitage 2001: 33).

For Virilio, cinematic technologies have bolstered their status in the sphere of art and aesthetics. To be sure, they are the central technologies in our ever more picnoleptic-based culture. Special effects such as "trick photography," which make visible what Virilio describes as the "supernatural" or the invisible, have supplanted paintings and sculptures as important artistic or aesthetic artifacts, as picnolepsy itself becomes a series of technical prostheses. These special effects produce huge quantities of supernatural images and employ the human imaginary to conjure up the impossible, to create picnolepsy, which is then used to assemble the "cheapest tricks"; and these, according to the early French film-maker Georges Méliès, "have the greatest impact," such as the "stop trick" that transforms one image into another (Virilio 2009a: 25–6). Virilio's contention here is exceptionally far-sighted regarding the changes that several theorists recognized as occurring in recent decades, particularly the impact of those technological special effects that fundamentally alter the appearance of reality. Without a doubt, the growing delegation of the human eye to cinematic technologies, and especially to the cinematographic motor's "power of breaking the methodical series of filmed instants [. . .] [of] regluing sequences and so suppressing all apparent breaks in duration," currently threatens to bring about a mass desynchronization and a mass picnoleptic disaster – or a kind of "black out" all over the world (p. 26). (For historical accounts of such developments, see Cubitt 2001 or Friedberg 2006.)

Virilio's key example of these sorts of events, taken from the 1970s, is the billionaire American movie mogul Howard Hughes (1905–76). At the age of 47 Hughes went into hiding until his death, making what was once visible invisible, because, Virilio claims, quoting the journalist James Phelan, Hughes became "*a man who couldn't stand being seen*" (2009a: 34). However, Hughes's imaginary had no wish for more money or cinematic success. Instead, he used his riches to "purchase total reclusion in a dark room" filled only with a movie screen, a cine-projector, and remote controls (pp. 34–6). The price of creating such cinematic special effects was negligible, as they could be purchased inexpensively in America. Yet Hughes, in making what was once visible invisible, was defending the commitment he had made to the force of his supernatural image, to advertising, and to the development of himself as a kind of special effect. In this situation, therefore, it was the famous picnoleptic idol, Hughes himself – his continuous teasing of his public so that it maintained its belief in him – that was the technical prosthesis or special effect. Hughes, who renounced watches, described himself as the "*Master of Time*," and he can thus be viewed as seeking an omnipotent picnolepsy, or as attempting to "win" in "the game of life" by creating a "dichotomy between the marks of his own personal time and those of astronomical time, so as to master whatever happens and fulfill immediately what is in the offing" (pp. 34–5). Hughes's attempt to invoke the impossible was never successful, which meant that this "*technological monk*" (p. 37) died alone among his special effects, non-natural supplements, and cheap tricks. But the fact that cinematic technologies could drive Hughes into disappearance until his demise – that making what was once visible invisible could wreak havoc on the human imaginary – demonstrates how culturally dominant the conjuring up of the impossible, of picnolepsy, has become.

A further point this example reveals is that photography, cinematic technologies, and picnolepsy are not separate from cultures of disappearance. Hence the changes in the condition of picnolepsy that are now occurring indicate a shift in the character of human culture, cognition, and perception. It is exactly this cultural change that is at issue in Virilio's essay on "the world as we see it" and its "passing" in *The Aesthetics of Disappearance*. The methodology he selects to examine the transformations in picnolepsy and cultural organization that shape the state of the postmodern age of the aesthetics of disappearance uses his concept of technical "prostheses of subliminal comfort."

TECHNICAL PROSTHESES OF SUBLIMINAL COMFORT, IMAGES, AND MASS INDIVIDUALISM

Virilio claims that there are two main features of the growth of picnolepsy. First, improvements in photography and

cinema have broader repercussions on culture, which is
evident from the case of Howard Hughes. The supernatural image, the making visible of the invisible, are connected
to issues regarding "cheap tricks," aesthetics, and the
human imaginary, and not only to issues of photographic
or cinematic invention as such. Generally this signifies that
improvements in the supernatural image have consequences
for further regions of culture. The second feature of the
growth of picnolepsy results from this condition, in that
there are diverse kinds of picnolepsy operating within culture. These have different standards according to which they
can be classified as helpful or accurate, and they have to be
analyzed by diverse methods.

In *The Aesthetics of Disappearance* Virilio argues that photography and cinema do not embody the whole of picnolepsy;
these two have always subsisted as a particular manifestation
of the wider "*fait accompli* of technology" (2009a: 51). For
Virilio, discourses concerning photography, cinema, and picnolepsy are actually discourses about the accomplished fact
of technology, which, for him, is "detached from [. . .] cultural preconceptions" and "desires to become the metaphor
of the world." Consider how the concept of "technology"
is increasingly linked to aesthetic studies, or how numerous
theoretical discourses today are effectively colonized by technology. Media history, for example, considers the cinematic
technologies of the past with growing interest; new media
studies contemplates more and more the technologization
of human vision; and, finally, cultural geography increasingly deliberates on diverse urban configurations and on
the impact of technology on city cultures. Similarly, photographic and cinematic images are transmitted by or through
types of technology that depict the human world. To exhibit
and validate their photographs or movies, photographers and
cinematographers are therefore compelled to transform their

perhaps once imaginary images into technological forms that show the results of their labors. Technology, for Virilio, thus amounts to a "revolution" in human consciousness and culture: it desires to replace our individual human expressions, attitudes, and ambitions with an "artificial condition."

Naturally, the different kinds of technology evoked by diverse discourses obey distinctive logics. The different discourses that comprise a culture's picnolepsy (photography and cinema, aesthetics, science, and so on) all display a diverse series of logics concerning "assisted" or "subliminal" images. In *The Aesthetics of Disappearance*, Virilio alludes to these distinctive discourses as relating to technical "prostheses of subliminal comfort" (2009a: 71) – a concept hereafter abbreviated throughout the book to "technical prostheses."

Virilio remarks that the logics of technical prostheses are associated with the "progress" of electronics and with an operative or "intelligent" neurosurgical tranquilization, which is effected through the implantation of spectators seeking subliminal comfort (p. 57). This signifies that the logics of specific technical prostheses such as computer or cinema screens are artificial and determined by our cultural preconceptions. Every synergy of human eye, computer screen, and cinematographic motor must therefore be considered as an effort to impose the annihilation of inborn human feelings through technical prostheses (p. 67). Consequently the logic of, for instance, computer screens is the logic of projection, of technical prostheses' "accelerated voyages, of which we are no longer even conscious" (p. 71). For Virilio, any change in the logic of the technologies of the screen alters the character of the projections of technical prostheses. Accordingly, all technical prostheses seek to bring about the obliteration of natural human sensations –in other words, to follow their own logics. However, this also means that technical prostheses are themselves susceptible to modification through other technical prostheses or as a result of the eradication of instinctive human feelings.

Virilio's argument here is that cultural ties are mediated by technical prostheses or by the endeavor to travel, at an accelerated rate and in audiovisual "vehicles" such as cinema, within the realm of a "false day" (ibid.). The very structure of human culture is made up of the images produced within it and the logics it develops to decide whether particular inherent human sensations are to be eliminated or sublimated. While different kinds of technical prostheses have diverse logics, distinct cultures have different forms of art, science, and subliminal images. We live as so-called "individuals" within this culture founded on a never ending succession of technical prostheses, whose diverse logics mediate who we are and what we become. Yet, Virilio maintains, contemporary "individuals" do not add up to a great deal because they are *"an effect of sensorial mass"* (p. 53), of the mass-media culture their senses are provided with. In other words, from the outset, postmodern "individuals" are predestined to be targets of the *fait accompli* of technology – of the countless technical prostheses all around them – and with regard to which they will inexorably arrange "their" everyday life (p. 51).

Systems of picnolepsy in culture thus establish what Virilio throughout his writings calls the trajectory of "mass individualism" – that is, individuals with apparently simulated personalities, thoughts, and ambitions. But how are we to comprehend such mass individualism, its culture and its organization of picnolepsy, its different technical prostheses, and their relationships? How do diverse cultures decide upon the importance and distinctiveness of the various ways of systematizing the technical prostheses that mediate them? Virilio's reply to these questions is that the organization of the *fait accompli* of technology and technical prostheses is accomplished by the technical beyond.

THE TECHNICAL BEYOND

The technical beyond specifies the "further side" of the logics of the *fait accompli* of technology and technical pros-theses. This indicates that the technical beyond systematizes technical prostheses and determines the "achievements" or "disappointments" of every image, as it inexorably imposes the extermination of innate human sensations. In *The Aesthetics of Disappearance* Virilio introduces three different technical beyonds and explains how they organize picnolepsy. The foundations of ancient cultures, of premodernity, and of modernity are, for Virilio, characterized by three kinds of organized technical beyonds. To appreciate why he describes the aesthetics of disappearance as an "irresistible project and projection toward a technical beyond" (2009a: 103), it is therefore helpful to comprehend what these technical beyonds are and how they operate.

Virilio argues that, from the first human cultures to today, technology has remained the typical mode of traditional picnolepsy (pp. 85–107). As an instance of the traditional type of technological systematization he presents Eve, the very first woman, who originally performs "the logistical role" later accomplished by "technical media" (p. 86). The "technology" that is woman adheres to a predetermined method for her own "seductive" escapades and for those of her spouse, Adam. Woman emerges with Satan, who materializes in the Bible as her seducer. But woman in turn seduces man, and so she begins both the technological and the reproductive cycle of humankind. Technology is thus forever transmitted from the past and conveyed to us in the present through our cultural preconceptions. Ancient technology, then, just like contemporary technology, creates prescribed images. Here the ends of technology, of woman, and of man's seduction by woman involve our "disappearance" or our "continued expulsion from the world" where we have previously existed, which, in the case of Adam and Eve, is of course the Garden of Eden. Through these images and through histori-cal awareness, technology connects itself with the original woman. Technology and woman therefore emerge jointly, while also linking history to the present day.

This type of technologization organizes the customs and systems of ancient female and male culture. Men and women participate in a chronological picnolepsy by way of the technology that is woman; they construct their mass individ-ualism as a community and arrange their culture using the logistical role of woman, who is permitted to seduce man and who, in turn, is seduced by this technology. For Virilio, the picnolepsy conveyed by this technological seduction deter-mines what woman must seduce in man in order to be his seducer, what man must let himself be seduced by in order to be seduced by technology, and what part both must per-form in relation to technology (ibid.). Every spectator and his or her cultural preconceptions are assigned a position in the system as the female seducer or as the man seduced by the female as technology, and the spectators' mass individual wants are fashioned by this system.

Virilio suggests that this is the kind of technical beyond and systematization that is traditional in ancient cultures. Contrary to this type, which is rooted in the association between history, the *fait accompli* of technology, and the present day, Virilio elucidates two other types of techni-cal beyond: the technical beyonds of premodernity and modernity. For Virilio, premodernity and modernity are characterized by their dependence upon technical beyonds that center on human movement. Their divergence from the ancient technical beyond of woman is marked by the fact that they are, as it were, "on the road" to a future where the dif-ficulties confronting human culture will be solved through mobilization. Virilio singles out two important forms of technical beyond in *The Aesthetics of Disappearance*: premodern "zoophilism" (love of animals) and, following a declaration by the French test pilot Jean-Marie Saget, the modern technical beyond of "flying into the unknown" (p. 102).

The idea of zoophilism stems from Virilio's philosophy of the 1980s and attains its most comprehensive development in *The Aesthetics of Disappearance* (pp. 95–6) and *Negative Horizon* (2005a: 39–78). In Virilio's influential historical work and philosophical thought, the premodern and modern forms of the aesthetics of disappearance find their clearest and most powerful formulations. For Virilio, the human world can be understood through philosophical reflection on zoophilism, which he describes as the "vehicular attraction of the coupling" (2009a: 96), and which precedes the invention of sophisticated technical objects. Zoophilism, then, produces "another form of heterosexuality." Virilio's reflections on zoophilism therefore reveal how the "horse in particular was treated like a god by the polemarch [warlord], even solemnly married" (p. 95). Zoophilism, thus illustrated by the horse and rider, is then a store of "power, source of speed in combat, but beyond that the zoophilous cult likes proposing the image of the hybrid animal:" The "bulls are winged or sphinxes have lions' bodies and human heads; later they are represented as winged and feminized" (p. 95) This implies that picnolepsy is not only continually in movement, but also that its objective is what Virilio calls the technical beyond. With the technical beyond, all contradictions and oppositions between humans and animals are resolved in a system of philosophical picnolepsy.

Virilio's fundamental idea regarding zoophilism is that human existence, much like animal existence, is characterized by a kind of "hidden wisdom" (ibid.), which moves through the dynamics of *escalation* or through the "metaphors" and "scenarios" of an ever intensifying picnolepsy (Kahn: 2010). Every one of the diverse technical prostheses is united with another, in the philosophical sense that they depict a world-wide trajectory of "annoying riddles to those on the road" of life. In Virilio's system, all picnolepsy is therefore connected. Indeed, for him, "true" picnolepsy is comprised of moving images integrated into the technical beyond of mass individualism, and this fact guarantees its allegiance to, and its total destruction by, subliminal images (pp. 95–101). In zoophilism, all potential images are combined in one technical beyond, and their "truth" and assimilation are evaluated in accordance with its logics. This explanation of zoophilism surfaces from Virilio's contention that "true" picnolepsy is a "total enigma," which denotes that the validity or speciousness of any image or technical prosthesis is determined by its connection to the total enigma that is the whole of picnolepsy.

The third kind of technical beyond is the modern one of "flying into the unknown." In contrast to zoophilism, where picnolepsy is the vehicular attraction of the coupling, this technical beyond depicts picnolepsy as possible to assimilate because, as Virilio puts it, it is the foundation of "going to the other side!" (p. 102). Indeed, as Virilio suggests (p. 102):

> There really is a technological donjuanism, a hijacking of machines that renews that of logistical spouses. The former triangle is completely modified and the rapport is established between a *unisex* (definitive dissimulation of physiological identities) and a technical vector, contact with the body of the loved one or of the territorial body disappearing usually as the dynamics of the passage intensify.

Now humanity is the conqueror of flight, both in the sense of "voyage" and in that of "escape." Everyone has an entitlement to blast off into vision technologies. This technical beyond commences for Virilio (pp. 101–2) with various developments, such as the women's revolution of the nine-teenth and twentieth centuries.

Woman, zoophilism, and "flying into the unknown" are the three crucial technical beyonds discussed in *The Aesthetics of Disappearance*. While there are important distinctions between them, there are also significant structural similari-ties. For example, in every technical beyond, all the diverse regions of picnolepsy are united in attaining an objective that is in movement, propelled onward into the future, or, put differently, regarded as the solution to the difficulties confronting culture. Within a technical beyond, all the cul-tural organizations such as science, cinema, or technology combine to struggle for a shared yet mobilized objective for humanity. Accordingly, picnolepsy obtains a task or a part to play in the further setting in motion of humanity.

However, for Virilio, the changes in picnolepsy that have occurred over the past two centuries have escalated the technical beyond of "flying into the unknown." Nowadays picnolepsy is organized intensively. In postmodern or postindustrial culture the problem of the subliminal image, of picnolepsy, is expressed in an accelerated language. The technical beyond has gained in authority, particularly the technical beyond of "flying into the unknown." Today, Virilio claims, picnolepsy is increasingly organized toward the satisfaction of worldwide technological, not of human, objec-tives. The aesthetics of picnolepsy is appreciated in terms of speed in our picnoleptic-powered global culture. It is this transmutation of picnolepsy, already indicated by the "irre-sistible project and projection toward a technical beyond," that defines Virilio's idea of the aesthetics of disappearance.

THE AESTHETICS OF DISAPPEARANCE

What, in that case, is the aesthetics of disappearance? For Virilio, the answer to this question rests in the global proliferation of technical prostheses, the accelerated growth of photography and film technologies since the nineteenth century, and the escalation of the modern technical beyond of "flying into the unknown." As he argues in the final chapter of *The Aesthetics of Disappearance* (2009a: 109–21), the irresistible project and projection toward the modern technical beyond has not been abandoned or overlooked, but intensified and accelerated. I will discuss the intensification and acceleration of the modern technical beyond in Chapter 2, which concentrates on Virilio's examination of cinema, war, and the logistics of perception. What is apparent in *The Aesthetics of Disappearance*, though, is that technical prostheses have become the powerhouse of picnolepsy, supernatural images, and the human imaginary in contemporary culture. In issues of what Virilio calls "technological donjuanism" and the "hijacking of machines that renews that of the logistical spouses" (p. 102) alike, photography, cinema, and the subliminal image machines of postmodern aesthetics are all anchored in maximizing the systemic logic and functioning of speed (pp. 109–10). This urge for acceleration is situated at the core of technical prostheses. Consequently, the goal of supernatural images and of the contemporary human imaginary is to render the creation and consumption of cinematographic visual impressions and the use of film ever more intense and faster, and thereby to optimize the possibilities for the camera's special effects.

For Virilio, the inexorable propagation of technical prostheses has intensified and accelerated traditional cultural ties by connecting nearly all of humanity in a modern technical beyond centered on movement. Beyond woman, zoophilism, and the vehicular attraction of the coupling, "going to the other side" – which is the objective of the technical beyond of "flying into the unknown" – increasingly has a universal attraction that it did not have under premodernity. This alters forever the character and position of picnolepsy in contemporary culture.

This transformation influences not merely supernatural images and the human imaginary, but also mass individualism itself. Situated within an array of technical prostheses that, more and more, adhere to one technical beyond, our "individuality" or "parapsychology" becomes ever more "electronic": we appear to "electrify" in the diffusion of technical prostheses (p. 53). Cultural ties are therefore gradually more artificial, connected by seemingly different and expanding, yet actually similar and therefore fewer devices, and shaped by the junction of innumerable technical prostheses that follow parallel logics. With the intensification and acceleration of the modern technical beyond, there is, to a greater extent, an integrated mass individualism that is in evidence in postmodern culture. Mass individualism is thus the nodal point where various related machines and aesthetic symbols come together as cultural links are intensified and accelerated. This transformative process is summarized by Virilio in *The Aesthetics of Disappearance*, where he maintains that the "main idea" of contemporary culture is "to put into question the sensorial categories in a general way, but especially from one individual to another, *to obtain an effect of sensorial mass*."

If we consider Virilio's declarations regarding the variations wrought by an increasingly accelerated culture and the concurrent escalation of modern types of "going to the other side," society, and mass individualism, several kinds of reactions are conceivable, such as that of the postmodern French philosopher Bernard Stiegler (2010: 171–80). Stiegler understands the modern technical beyond as the project of "telecracy" or "the real time of live communications and [. . .] the just-in-time adjustment of politics to public opinion, which has, as a consequence, become an *audience*"

(p. 172). Yet he seeks to curtail the modern technical beyond and to advance the goals of democracy through the use of the very same accelerated communications technologies, as "the only possible way to invent new forms of social bond and civil peace" (p. 177). This can only be accomplished, he contends, by endeavoring to attain true democracy through new techno-social associations, organizations, and movements that will confront what he calls the "unprecedented political and social collapse" triggered by the escalation of the modern technical beyond.

Virilio's objective, contrary to Stiegler's, is to problematize the modern technical beyond from the standpoint of aesthetics. For example, Virilio argues that the progressively worldwide conception of the women's revolutions' "flying into the unknown," away from the "beauty" and "corsetry" of the nineteenth and twentieth centuries, offers a militarized and accelerated foundation for the sociocultural and political phenomenon that is "the liberation of women" through the emancipation of "the seductions of technique" (2009a: 101). From the twentieth century onwards, then, women could "go for sports records" or "climb aboard fast machines," their "new corset-armature" in the shape of the airplane or automobile cockpit. Accordingly, Virilio claims that it is imperative to reveal the globalization of technical prostheses through a focus on their growing intensification and speed. Because technical prostheses are associated with mass individualism, he suggests that the narrower the scope is of ever more similar technical prostheses that are based on subliminal images within contemporary culture, the more closed and limited that culture is turning out to be. The chief danger confronting the age of the aesthetics of disappearance is the relegation of picnolepsy to a solitary technique whose only principle is acceleration. Virilio appreciates technical prostheses as sophisticated apparatuses that draw us into themselves, automating us as picnolepsy is increasingly assessed with regard to technological special effects and to its trajectories of speed. The huge danger of technical prostheses, in Virilio's eyes, is their ability to consign us to their own systems of acceleration and innovation, militarization, and mobilization, wherein our only choice is to assimilate our bodies to vision technologies – in other words, to disappear. The risk confronting human-centered picnolepsy, a picnolepsy without technological special effects, is that it, too, will vanish, as machines and their special effects are not only advocated but also cherished by mass individualism.

Nevertheless, the age of the aesthetics of disappearance is also an age where all questions remain open (Virilio 2009b: 54). Clearly, Virilio is not going to suggest a new, perhaps postmodern, technical beyond to substitute that of the modern flight into the unknown because, for him, technical prostheses are complex machines that incorporate their own means of escalation. He maintains that ideas such as Stiegler's concerning democracy and technology are not practicable ways of "going to the other side" because the accelerated assimilation of the human body to vision technologies is today considered both fashionable and commendable. Detractors should therefore attain a conception and a critical practice of "going to the other side" that eschew those of philosophers like Stiegler, in their efforts to reinvigorate democracy by means of new techno-social associations. Rather, such a critical practice must concentrate on our ability to critique the technological "nothingness" of the so-called "reality" of virtual reality, for instance. For the fact is that such technological voids relegate everything to the principle of speed (Virilio 2009a: 119). Moreover, once the modern technical beyond has become "the supreme goal of technique," we are left merely with a limited variety of ever more similar technical prostheses. Accordingly, the goal of aesthetic critical practice must be to critique the pursuit of "going to the other side" by focusing on activities such as the breaking of "land speed records," which regard "as primordial the reaction of the milieu to the object's form-in-movement and vice-versa."

As a prototype for this critical practice, Virilio explains how innovations in modern aerodynamics and land speed records have the possibility to change the character of temporality and of picnolepsy by unlocking new accelerated technical prostheses. One instance of these changes is the literal unearthing by Craig Breedlove, holder of the world land speed record in 1965, of "a time that would no longer be one" (ibid.). Here, as Breedlove suggests, *"one simply exists"* in "a time that would be on earth yet nowhere," since one is left only with "highways" concerned with "pleasure and violation of limits" (ibid.). Breedlove's automobile-induced ecstasy thus initiates a new technical prosthesis (the smoothing out and effective destruction of the world) into photographic and cinematic discourses that change the way they depict the world.

Virilio suggests that this kind of aerodynamic and accelerated, photographic, and cinematic exploration conjures up a paradigm of the subliminal image that has everything to do with exploiting the total logic and performance of speed, and yet has as its starting point the annihilation of time and space, understood as "chorography" (ibid.). By chorography – which he describes as "a figure of the road-building surge of Empires," as distinct from "geography" or "the mere mapping out" of territory – Virilio is getting at how technical prostheses tend to impose the eradication of natural human feelings concerning space and time in particular. For extant technical prostheses have the capability to escalate their own logics, or to introduce new versions of themselves – as in the case of the train and automobile revolutions of the nineteenth and twentieth centuries. In this way new technical prostheses are continually being developed. With the inauguration of the train, or of Breedlove's supercar, for instance, the logics of sleek and speeding, photographic, and cinematic investigation have to change in response to these transformations, thereby disrupting what was until then a "common conception of space and time" (p. 120). Hence Virilio is arguing that techniques of picnolepsy are constantly being escalated (pp. 119–20). Certainly, with chorography it is essential to hypothesize the reality of an aesthetics that, by way of newly spatialized and temporalized lifestyles, escalates both our appetite and aptitude for "cultural innovation" (p. 120). This aesthetics is revealed in the spread of new interpretations of time for understanding the railroad and the highway, or in plans to set up new logics of "network schedules," which expand our "complex interconnections" and thus open up new areas of research and cultural development regarding technical prostheses, photography, and cinema. This aesthetics that escalates our faculties of cultural innovation is fundamental to Virilio's media theory. Assuming numerous diverse forms in his writings on the media, this escalated aesthetics will be connected, in subsequent chapters of this book, to concepts such as the logistics of perception, the vision machine, the city of panic, and the Museum of Accidents. Yet this aesthetics that escalates is, for Virilio, not just a set of picnoleptic techniques such as the modern technical beyond of "flying into the unknown" or the globalization of technical prostheses, but also an escalated aesthetics that remains open to aesthetic questioning – to an escalated critical practice. The goal of the following chapters is thus to consider how the media theory and critical practice of Virilio the "revelationary" rather than the revolutionary (2009b: 43) locate and conceptualize the notion of an escalated aesthetics of disappearance.

CONCLUSION

In *The Aesthetics of Disappearance*, Virilio's essay on "the world as we see it" and its "passing," Virilio considers how the character and condition of picnolepsy have altered in contemporary culture. He contends that, following woman and zoophilism, the modern technical beyond of "flying into the unknown" currently organizes picnolepsy, classifies visual understanding for us, and guides us toward the objective of a movement that has only intensified and accelerated its authority in the age of the aesthetics of disappearance. These days, what governs aesthetics as an organizing criterion is the principle of speed and of special effects proliferated by technical prostheses operating within postmodern global culture. In submitting this argument, Virilio expounds a method for the examination of picnolepsy through technical prostheses and the technical beyond, which offer techniques and logics for deciding which kinds of image are subliminal and which are not in specific areas of picnolepsy or technological experience. Rather than downgrading everything to the level of issues of acceleration and special effects, he makes an important case for paying attention to the annihilation of our own "unique historical time" and of our own unique historical space wrought by technical prostheses, and accordingly for the key role that the "revelation" of these increasingly global systems and institutions performs at present (2009a: 120). To attain this possibility for revelation, he claims that it is critical to concentrate on concepts and practices such as chorography, on organizations and issues relating to travel, practices of speed, movement, and transportation, or on the question of the modern technical beyond, which, like the simple railroad carriage compartment, is also, for its passengers, a technical prosthesis that annihilates time and space.

2

CINEMA, WAR, AND THE LOGISTICS
OF PERCEPTION

INTRODUCTION

This chapter examines Virilio's most important illustration of the aesthetics of disappearance in order to consider
various results he obtains from it for the contemplation of
cinema and war. It discusses Virilio's philosophy of a militarized aesthetics of disappearance, and it also elucidates the
connections that he makes between cinema, war, the modern
technical beyond of "flying into the unknown," and the
"logistics of perception."

CINEMA, WAR, AND THE AESTHETICS OF
DISAPPEARANCE

Cinema – both moving films and the entire network of institutions and people engaged with film production – indicates,
for Virilio, an instant of technological and psychological
shock comparable to that of weaponry. Cinema is, therefore,

a doorway to his media theory of modern and postmodern war (see Virilio 1989, 2000b, 2002a). Virilio argues that war and the techno-psychology of shock that is cinema have cultivated a deadly mutual dependence. But how can we consider such lethal interdependence? What does cinema do to media theory and to war? And what kinds of media theory or war are feasible after the invention of cinema?

Virilio's examination of these questions in *War and Cinema: The Logistics of Perception* (1989) commences, however, not with the birth of cinema itself, but with the case proposed by that Nazi *cinéaste* and minister of propaganda under the Third Reich, Paul Joseph Goebbels, who, during World War II, initially tried to ban the showing of films in color to the German populace. This "patron" of the German cinema "banned the showing of the first film in Agfacolor, *Women Are Better Diplomats*, on the grounds that the color was depressing and of wretched quality" (Virilio 1989: 8). By contrast with "American Technicolor," Virilio notes, "the German process struck Goebbels as nothing short of *shameful*." He indicates how, later, Agfacolor's new color stock was enhanced and how "it enjoyed enormous success in occupied Europe":

> In 1943, to mark ten years of Nazi cinema and the twenty-fifth anniversary of UFA [Universal Aktion Film], J. von Baky solemnly presented *The Adventures of Baron Münchhausen*, a high-budget Agfacolor film with a large number of very accomplished special effects. (1989: 8)

For Goebbels's wartime double anniversary of Nazi cinema, then, the only UFA film acceptable for showing was one concerning the escapades of a well-known fictional fanta-sist, and this film was given the expensive Agfacolor film treatment, complete with numerous consummate special effects. Nevertheless, Virilio reminds us that UFA "had been founded during the First World War, in 1917, and that in the following year it became the main [state and arms industry subsidized] complex of cinematographic production, distribution, and development in wartime Germany" (ibid.). "At the height of total war," therefore, "it seemed to Goebbels and to Hitler himself that the rescuing of German cinema from black-and-white would provide it with a competitive edge against the tonic power of American productions."

Concentrating on how a Nazi *cinéaste* banned the screening of films in Agfacolor to the German public is perhaps a strange opening for a book on war or cinema. After all, there is considerable historical evidence concerning this "patron" of the German cinema, and the contentions of those who sought to ban the showing of the first film in Agfacolor have correctly been disclosed as politically motivated and technologically determined (Tegel 2007). So what is Virilio attempting to accomplish by writing about Goebbels's quarrel with American Technicolor?

Virilio's argument is, primarily, a comparative one. It invites readers to consider the problem of how to react to a war over national cinematic processes, and it does so by evoking Goebbels's contentions, which obviously aimed to refute the idea of American technological superiority. Additionally, it shows the capability of national shame to "improve" Agfacolor stock, and it introduces the question of whether military success may or may not be tied to cinematic success. Equally significantly, however, it permits Virilio to broach numerous issues about the nature of war, politics, and writings on cinema generally. Certainly he gives no credibility to Goebbels's standpoint. Nonetheless, his position concerning Goebbels's thinking exposes several possible inadequacies of conventional theoretical explanations of cinema financing, war, and filmic special effects. Virilio claims that film and war are linked not only to the state and to the arms industry, but also to cinematographic color, and that the "powerful mimetic faculty of wartime American cinema" in particular "was a kind of perceptual luxury" that was "quite distinct from other forms of spectacle and entertainment" (1989: 8–9). Indeed, for Virilio, cinema is an intangible yet recurrent indulgence that we find it increasingly difficult to forgo.

Virilio argues that the Nazi leaders appreciated cinema extremely well: "they placed actors and directors under military discipline right from the outbreak of hostilities, any absence from the studios being regarded as an act of desertion and punished accordingly" (p. 9). Yet the shift from monochrome to color to compete against the tonic power of American productions was not Goebbels's and Hitler's only problem with German cinema. For they also "had a contemptuous relationship with the cinema people," many of whom were not Nazis, but communists and/or Jews; and these finally met a tragic end, by suicide or deportation to Nazi concentration camps.

We might object at this point that Virilio rehashes or exaggerates well-worn connections between war and cinema. Film historians, for example, have long recorded the coercive ways in which costly German movies continued to be made until the end of World War II. Moreover, it is well known that these final pictures were still being projected in the remaining Nazi citadels even when many cinemas in the cities of the Third Reich were being bombed by the Allies (Winkel and Welch 2010). But this is not all that is at issue. In fact, Virilio is making a more multifaceted argument, which extends far beyond such concerns. Goebbels and Hitler, he suggests, even when "staring military collapse in the face," still wanted their movies to be the "greatest of all time, spectacular epics outrivaling the most sumptuous American super-productions" (1989: 9). Hence, in his estimation, during World War II something new occurred in cinema, and this was the Germans' growing "obsession with the American perceptual arsenal." Not only was there an effort to read America's magazines and newspapers, correspondence, and the international press, but there was also an attempt to surpass its filmic universe. Simultaneously, within the United States, the production and circulation of propaganda movies was increasingly commandeered by the military. Furthermore, somewhat surprisingly, Spanish surrealist film directors such as "Luis Buñuel could be found in 1942 shooting documentaries for the US Army, while Frank Capra moved from his inter-war satires (most notably with Harry Langdon) to the ponderous didacticism of *Why We Are Fighting* (1942–45)" (pp. 9–10). Even more blatant were "the songs and dances of Fred Astaire," which were merely "disguised calls for a new mobilization" (p. 10).

Yet, beyond any proof or data that can be cited concerning the "aggressive colors" of these American films, frequently regarded by Europeans as signs of American vulgarity, there is an "energy of the visible" radiating from them, an energy of the visible given out from the United States itself, which "made them into veritable 'war paintings'" (p. 10; Virilio 2009b: 60, 2012: 61). If we focus on the cinema of World War II, Virilio claims, in effect, on the aesthetics of disappearance, this energy of the visible can be characterized as a form of "logistics," as a kind of perceptual, militarized, and immediate "charge," in the sense of "excitement" or "arousal." The mission of this energy of the visible was to supply and instill cinema audiences with new military vigor, instantly to transform and "wrench them out of apathy in the face of danger or distress, to overcome that wide-scale demoralization which was so feared by generals and statesmen alike" (1989: 10). However, American film, like war, is not simply one more magical "capacity for movement" – as Virilio calls both film and war – in the ongoing history of human perception. It is also directly linked to total war and to the economy. Put differently, following World War II and the dropping of atomic bombs by the United States and its Allies on Japan, at Hiroshima and Nagasaki, in 1945, Virilio investigates the politico-economic and cultural repercussions on modern and postmodern war and cinema of the full flowering of the aesthetics of disappearance. In Virilio's interpretation, cinema, war, and the aesthetics of disappearance become the basis for a new sort of media theory, for a barely describable wartime sadness directed at a future that might yet require an examination of cinematic destruction, a deliberation on the endurance of the aesthetics of disappearance, and lessons in grief amid the no longer mediated or theoretical debris of nuclear war. Beyond World War II and the Cold War, the Korean, Vietnam, Gulf, Kosovo, and Iraq Wars, all of which, of course, remain militarily vital, the now ageing German and US wartime propaganda films nevertheless continue as a form of logistics. As such, these films are a kind of perceptual, militarized, and instantaneous "charge" to be experienced by today's masses, from the United States and Europe to Latin America, Africa, and Asia, many of which find themselves seized by and responding to the terror and legacies of nuclear war.

THE AESTHETICS OF DISAPPEARANCE, CINEMA, AND THE ESCALATION OF THE MODERN TECHNICAL BEYOND OF "FLYING INTO THE UNKNOWN"

The interpretations of cinema in Virilio's writings investigate the impact cinema has had on war and present-day cultural existence. For Virilio (1989: 11), cinema and war are not just capacities for movement that have long passed by their respective nineteenth-century and ancient development, following which military psychology and physiology, or perhaps the inventor Etienne-Jules Marey's chrono-photographic rifle, "which allowed its user to aim at and photograph an object moving through space," can carry on as before. Rather, if we are to theorize cinema, particularly following Marey's military research into movement, then that theorization has to change. In a significant chapter from *War and Cinema*, "Cinema Isn't I See, It's I Fly" (pp. 11–30), Virilio explains the influence of cinema on the concept of aerialized war.

Our feeling for cinema, the methods by which we systematize and elucidate our perception, are all essential to mass individualism, to its cultural preconceptions, to its understanding of itself and others, and also to aerialized war. The history of cinematic technologies thus relates the narrative of how we became weaponized; it situates our current weaponization as a component of a photographic continuity and indicates our likely chronophotographic or weaponized futures. Such cinematic technologies can thus be understood as resembling the logics of targeting and, like the technology of photography, they can take numerous physical, moving, and spatial forms. In "Cinema Isn't I See, It's I Fly," Virilio explains some of these forms. In fact, he associates them with the most important wars, inventions, and weapons of the past century and a half, including battlefield observation balloons, balloons outfitted with an aerial-mapping telegraph, camera-kites, camera-pigeons, camera-balloons, chronophotography, and cinematography aboard small reconnaissance aircraft. Indeed,

[b]y 1967 the US Air Force had the whole of South-East Asia covered, and pilotless aircraft would fly over Laos and

send their data back to IBM centres in Thailand or South Vietnam. *Direct vision was now a thing of the past*: in the space of a hundred and fifty years, the target area had become a cinema "location," the battlefield a film set out of bounds to civilians. (1989: 11)

Contemporary attitudes to cinema are therefore bound to systems of war and military values, each laboring toward its own totalizing, aerialized, and data-led idea of indirect vision. Examples that Virilio provides in this chapter include World War I, where "D. W. Griffith was the only American [civilian] film-maker authorized to go to the front to shoot propaganda footage for the Allies" (pp. 11–13; see also Virilio 2002a: 87–8). Additional illustrations involve the targeted late nineteenth-century "motion demonstrations" of Billy Bitzer, in which he bound his cine-camera to the "location" of "the buffers of a locomotive traveling at full speed"; the German film director Carl Dreyer, who strove to "create an *artificial* unity of time by means of a *real* unity of place, and thereby illustrating Walter Benjamin's observation about a kind of cinema which was able to 'present an object for simultaneous collective experience, as it was possible for architecture at all times'"; and, finally, at the close of the nineteenth century, "Oskar Messter, not having a camera," using "the room in which he lived as a camera obscura by blacking it out and leaving only a tiny hole at the street side" (Virilio 1989: 11–13).

In *The Aesthetics of Disappearance* Virilio explains these processes of systematizing cinema in relation to the conceptualization of a movement or escalation to indirect vision – to, in fact, the modern technical beyond of "flying into the unknown" discussed in Chapter 1. This modern technical beyond has been the coordinating principle for major wars, innovations, and weapons systems since the nineteenth century. Yet, as Virilio stresses (2009a: 85–107), the modern technical beyond of "flying into the unknown" is not, in truth, an age of technical ideas, but instead a form of technical thinking or projection to the "far side" of the known, a mode of thought that can be portrayed through the concept of zoophilism or through the indirect vision of the modern technical beyond of "flying into the unknown." Besides, as he claims in the same book, in the era of the aesthetics of disappearance this technical beyond has increased its effectiveness and can now project its sensibilities globally. This denotes that the meanings of cinema enclosed within this technical beyond must be reconsidered in the age in question; and this is what the chapter "Cinema Isn't I See, It's I Fly," at least in part, endeavors to accomplish. Consequently Virilio reflects on the question of how fighters in World War I were organized to kill enemy soldiers without seeing "whom they were killing, since others had now taken responsibility for seeing in their stead" (1989: 14). "What," he asks, "was this abstract zone that Apollinaire accurately described as the site of a blind, non-directional desire?" This is a very important question regarding any effort to debate the political and cultural relationships, for instance, among the soldiers themselves, who could identify this abstract zone "only by the flight-path of their bullets and shells [. . .]." For here was "a kind of telescopic tensing toward an imagined encounter, a 'shaping' of the partner-cum-adversary before his probable fragmentation" (p. 15). His response to these questions is that we should persist in paying attention to how sight is organized and how it "lost its direct quality," how it "reeled out of phase" and how "the soldier had the feeling of being not so much destroyed as derealized or dematerialized," with "any sensory point of reference suddenly vanishing in a surfeit of optical targets."

"Cinema Isn't I See, It's I Fly" provides numerous

explanations as to why humanity is increasingly structured around such an awareness of cinematic seeing. It catalogs the various developments of the modern technical beyond of "flying into the unknown," and it alludes to their capacities for movement in the twentieth century that have hurled them into overdrive. Virilio thus offers many capacities for movement that have become a veritable "logistics of perception" (his expression for the military provision of imagery which, from World War I onwards, developed into the counterpart of the military provision of ammunition, thus establishing a new weapons system derived from the amalgamation of means of war transportation and cameras), thanks to the way in which they escalate the logics upon which the modern technical beyond of "flying into the unknown" is set up (pp. 21–5). For example, he argues that the artilleryman's attitude and logic of thought became equivalent to the camera operator's regarding the understanding of reality: the use of "lighting reveals everything" (p. 15). Hence by 1914, through the utilization of lighting for military–cinematic movement and escalation, the reality and "rationality" of anti-aircraft artillery was such that guns were being combined with searchlights to form "camera-machineguns." Here, then, the logistics of perception becomes unreal or irrational as it escalates into an indirect or cinematic vision of warfare. Likewise, in "refining and often misusing" the then revolutionary concept of the *carello* or "traveling shot," early film-makers such as Giovanni Pastrone "showed that the camera's function was less to produce images [. . .] than to manipulate and falsify dimensions" (p. 16). The traveling shot thus confirmed that "the first difference between cinema and photography is that the viewpoint can be mobile [. . .] and share the speed of moving objects." After Pastrone, therefore, what was confirmed "'false' in cinema was no longer the effect of accelerated perspective but the very depth itself, the temporal distance of the projected space." Lastly, years afterwards, he argues, "the electronic light of laser holography and integrated-circuit computer graphics would confirm this relativity in which speed appears as the primal magnitude of the image and thus the source of its depth." All of these instances corroborate the important coordinating principle of the modern technical beyond of "flying into the unknown," verifying the system by which it shapes its construction of a cinematic movement or escalation toward a model of indirect vision.

These capacities for movement, for "cinematic self-propulsion" (p. 17), thus become so many "logistics" or symbols of the power and accomplishments of the connections between cinematic vision and every important aerialized war, technical advance, and development in arms since the mid-nineteenth century. The basic values of the modern technical beyond of "flying into the unknown" are confirmed by its capacity for movement, by its "fleeting aerial perspective," which Virilio calls "dromoscopic": a speeding escalation that indicates the potentialities of the age of the aesthetics of disappearance, of the era in which vision, cinema, and aviation become one. The question he implicitly broaches in the chapter is: how are we to challenge the authority and activities of the modern technical beyond of "flying into the unknown"? He contends that, by 1914, there were numerous possibilities and, in choosing among them, humanity decided on aviation as "the ultimate way of *seeing*." Indeed, "contrary to what is generally thought, the air arm grew out of the reconnaissance services, its military value having initially been questioned by the general staffs." This is why the concept of an age of the aesthetics of disappearance can apply simultaneously, for example, to the different imaging techniques of reconnaissance aircraft and to the supplying of mobile ground troops with visual information. In other words, the escalation of the modern technical beyond of "flying into the unknown" through its capacity, say, to manage and mobilize artillery barrages, or to take photographs, compels a reassessment of the purpose and organization of cinematic investigation. Yet the aesthetics of disappearance, cinema, and war studies assume numerous diverse forms, according to the philosophical and military ideas and aims of the media theorist. How, then, should we approach and, more importantly, challenge the modern technical beyond of "flying into the unknown" and the logistics of perception? Prior to relating Virilio's explanation of the aesthetics of disappearance and of the logistics of perception, I shall delineate another important postmodern examination of cinema and the aesthetics of disappearance, which will serve as a helpful contrast to Virilio's investigation.

CINEMA AND THE AESTHETICS OF DISAPPEARANCE: JEAN BAUDRILLARD

Like Virilio, Jean Baudrillard (1929–2007) famously contemplated the transformations of cinema, technology, and the investigation of reality and history in the present period (Coulter 2010: 6–20). Baudrillard suggests that the significance of considering cinema lies in its relation to the primitive enjoyment that is the aesthetics of disappearance. Nevertheless, he does so from a different, almost anthropological, viewpoint and with goals that diverge from those of Virilio (Gane 2000: 77–87). Indeed, Baudrillard argues for a turn to a postmodern examination of cinema, and he asserts that there is "a kind of brute fascination" with cinema that is "unencumbered by aesthetic, moral, social, or political judgements" (Baudrillard 2000: 450).

And, as we shall see, as a postmodern media theorist, Baudrillard contends that familiarity with cinema is vital for any deliberation on the cultural politics of aerialized war. Actually, he insists on the need to consider the concept of cinema as immoral, as a postmodern technical beyond whose analytical or primary political power resides in this immorality. Hence, cinematic moving images,

> above and beyond all moral or social determination [. . .] are sites of the *disappearance* of meaning and representation, sites in which we are caught quite apart from any judgement of reality, thus sites of a fatal strategy of denegation of the real and of the reality principle. (Ibid.)

Put differently, for Baudrillard, a consideration of the postmodern technical beyond is imperative if we are to reflect on the cultural politics of moving images and cinema with a view to understanding how they simultaneously disappear yet somehow meaningfully occupy and represent our real, if increasingly indirect, everyday visual lives.

In the text under discussion here, which is the important lecture "The Evil Demon of Images," Baudrillard explains the aesthetics of disappearance and its culture of mushrooming images as a turn toward a possibly never ending cinematic theory that relishes a conception of cinema images as meaningless, multiplying, and out of control (ibid.). For the aesthete of disappearance, he claims, cinema has become accelerated through images. Both the foundation of our culture and the foundation of our aerialized wars, cinema, video, and digital representations mirror our fascination with images (pp. 450–1). So, for instance, the movie *The Last Picture Show* (1971) portrays a 1950s' vision of American manners and the atmosphere of small-town USA. But what makes audiences, especially European ones, feel somewhat doubtful is that the film is "a little too good, better adjusted, better than the others, without the sentimental, moral, and psychological tics of the films of that period" (p. 451). Baudrillard, then, is surprised at his discovery that *The Last Picture Show* "is a 1970s film, a perfectly nostalgic, brand new, retouched, a hyperrealist restitution of a 50s film."

For Baudrillard, these are some of the essential problems of the aesthetics of disappearance. In a culture of postmodern remakes, cinema is nothing but films that are "better than those of the period" they imitate (ibid.). The point of his lecture is therefore to evaluate the aesthetics of disappearance as indicating the defeat of the cinematic imaginary and to advocate a shift to a postmodern analysis of the simulated objects of the modern technical beyond.

Baudrillard's (1995, 2005) other relevant writings pursue a similar (although not an identical) course. He perceives the aesthetics of disappearance during the Gulf War of 1991 between the United States and its allies and Iraq, for example, as practically effacing the very possibility of contemplating cinema, or the mass media, as any kind of modern technical beyond. Thus Baudrillard's work during the 1990s implicitly represents critiques of the aesthetics of disappearance, such as Virilio's, as rather ineffectual when faced with the delirium-inducing simulated or virtual cinematic imagery of the postmodern Gulf War. In *The Gulf War Did Not Take Place* he proposes that, during the war, he was "reminded of *Capricorn One*," the film in which "the flight of a manned rocket to Mars, which only took place in a desert studio, was relayed live to all the television stations in the world" (Baudrillard 1995: 61). In other words, cinema and the mass media, considered by Virilio as depictions of movement toward picnolepsy and indirect vision (what he identifies as the modern technical beyond of "flying into the unknown"), for Baudrillard have turned actual aerialized war into its virtual double. Indeed, by means of the accelerated and increasingly sophisticated capacities for movement in operation during the Gulf War, the Iraqis, according to Baudrillard, were simply depicted "as a computerized target," while the United States' concealed satellite information merely gave the impression of an instantaneous "clean war" whose overriding purpose was in fact aimed at satisfying American duplicity (p. 62). (Baudrillard's own depiction, or orientalist "hollowing out," of the Iraqis and Islam during the Gulf War has been constructively critiqued by Almond (2009: 1–12).) In the era of the aesthetics of disappearance and cinematics, virtual war, and television screens, argues Baudrillard,

> everything tends to go underground, including information in its informational bunkers. Even war has gone underground in order to survive. In this forum of war which is the Gulf, everything is hidden: the planes are hidden, the tanks are buried, Israel plays dead, the images are censored and all information is blockaded in the desert: only TV functions as a medium without a message, giving at last the image of pure television. (1995: 63)

Contemporary cinematics and the mass media thus render all capacities for movement immediately subterranean and instantaneously informationalized, as they shift inevitably underground, toward new military formations or further interments. Through such capacities for movement and with the accelerated aerial war in the Gulf apparently screening everything ("the planes are hidden"), neither war's survival nor any sense of its reality is guaranteed today. War somehow "disappears" into the endless increase of interconnected tanks and entombments, as cinematics and the mass media gorge uncontrollably on the military's perspective and propaganda, disguised as explanation. In this paradoxical upsurge of military hardware and mediated "discussion," where speeding US jets and Iraqi tanks appear to be only mirages or the equivalent of a buried treasure, the reality of whole countries' capacity for movement vanishes, leaving media audiences shocked, yet fascinated with the endlessly repeated, "US military approved," and simulated if instantly unmemorable cinematic images. For, as Baudrillardian scholars Toffoletti and Grace (2010) argue, when cinema and the terror of war are drained of their symbolic qualities, the outcome is audience indifference. Here is also the root of Baudrillard's (1995: 63) infamous "hypothesis" that the Gulf War "would not" and "did not take place" – as, for Baudrillard, the simultaneously and ostensibly unrestrained yet actually suppressed media reporting, alongside the stunning deployment of imagery and information that appeared to show no injuries, blacked out an entire desert. For Baudrillard, then, the incessantly multiplying speculations, rival explanations, and TV images put forward by media "experts" with air time and space to fill heralded the age of the "medium without a message," the age and image of "pure" TV, in which hyper-efficient arms industry weaponry and simulations, US military misinformation, and "reality" combined to produce an ultimately "hidden" war.

THE AESTHETICS OF DISAPPEARANCE AND THE LOGISTICS OF PERCEPTION

Against Baudrillard's hypotheses, Virilio argues for the importance of persevering with the endeavor to reflect on cinema and to write about it despite the escalation of the modern technical beyond. Unlike Baudrillard, he is not suggesting a turn to a postmodern analysis of the simulated objects of the modern technical beyond. Therefore Virilio does not argue for erasing the very possibility of contemplating cinema as a kind of modern technical beyond. Indeed, for Virilio, the work of the critic of the art of technology is not to conjure up some new technical beyond subsequent to that of "flying into the unknown." Rather, it is to revisit repeatedly those capacities for movement that have produced contemporary conflicts, postmodern mass culture, and national sentiments, in order to discover in them our obsession with perceptual arsenals and our continual attempts to surpass those that already exist.

To continue to discuss cinema following the escalation of the modern technical beyond, Virilio turns again to his own media theory. At this point he develops an explanation of cinema and aerialized war that persists in imagining them as interdependent rather than merely as a haphazard sequence of unconnected capacities for movement. However, he simultaneously repudiates the creation of a "dromoscopic" or accelerated account of cinematic movement or military escalation, which is the heart of the modern technical beyond. This, then, situates his account of cinema and aerialized war somewhere else than Baudrillard's cinematic and media-centered hyperreality, and his turn to an understanding of the postmodern Gulf War as one that did not take place. What permits this idea that cinema and aerialized war are interdependent without making it into a modern technical beyond is Virilio's distinction between notions of actual space and time, which concern explicitly "old" modes of direct representation, and technologically revolutionary concepts that perform an aerial reconnaissance role. For the latter are modes of indirect vision or disappearance involving instantaneous or "real-time" information. In other words, for Virilio cinema and aerialized war, movement and escalation are all ideas that create the system wherein particular physiological objects such as our own actual bodies are often forgotten, as their "traces" become accessible to a host of new capacities for movement such as vibration sensors, cameras, and thermo-graphic pictures that identify objects by their temperature, and so on. In short, as time-lags are lost in real time, real time itself breaks the constraints of chronology and becomes cinematic. The aim of Virilio's consideration of cinema and aerialized war is thus to broach the issue of how military information allows the past or the future to be interpreted and how human activity, its heat and light, can be extrapolated and escalated in time and space as specific capacities for movement.

Virilio maintains that, without a conception of the escalation of cinema and aerialized war, our exploits in this realm would merely seem to be a directionless path, involving for instance the fitting of spotlights under bomber wing-tips or landing gear. He argues that the link between cinema, aerialized war, and capacities for movement must be underpinned by an awareness of the problem of combining technology and chronology, cinematics, military weaponry, warfare, speed, motorization, and firepower (1989: 19). To put it differently, if we cannot debate the relations between diverse capacities for movement in cinema and aerialized war, all we are left with are the seemingly subversive effects their actions produce on us and weapons, human perception, aesthetic form, and creativity.

When Virilio endeavors to explain this problem of "the technical mix" in "Cinema Isn't I See, It's I Fly," he contends that the significant thing is not to enter into a discussion about cinema *or* aerial war. Rather, as he also suggests in *Desert Screen: War at the Speed of Light*, war has always been "linked to perceptual phenomena" (2002a: 45). For Virilio, then, cinema and aerialized war are involved with the importance of perceptual yet militarized representation, or with the militarization of aesthetics. His stance on cinema and aerialized war, unlike that of the modern technical beyond, is concerned with the escalation of the problem of the technical mix and indirect vision, since for him these give rise to an interdependent drive toward an increasingly militarized technical beyond. What is needed, therefore, is an understanding of the implications of the fact that "the pilot's hand automatically trips the camera shutter with the same gesture that releases his weapon" (1989: 20; see also 2002a: 54). As indicated by Virilio, this understanding must take the form of assessing the implications of the capacities for movement that function in relation to cinema, logistics, and escalation.

Virilio situates such capacities for movement, which function as a logistics of perception, in the relation between war, weaponry, and the human eye, which took place at the beginning of the twentieth century, at the time when air forces were cultivating their armed philosophy. What, he argues, is vital about these capacities for movement is not their individual relation to war, the lightning advances of military weaponry and technology, and the human eye, but their combined relation to the "violent cinematic disruption of the space continuum" (1989: 20). For the growing interdependence between war, weaponry, and the human eye "literally exploded the old homogeneity of vision and replaced it with the heterogeneity of perceptual fields." As he writes in *Strategy of Deception*: the "logistics of perception *on all fronts* has won out over the logistics of weapons targeted along a particular front" (2000b: 24). What acts as a form of logistics, of the need to escalate, in such capacities for movement is not the individual militarized, weaponized, or human visual actions themselves, but the "explosion" metaphors that they collectively engender in those who are immediately involved in art and politics. The fact that film-makers "who survived the war [*sc.* World War I] moved without any break in continuity from the battlefield to the production of newsreels or propaganda features and then 'art films'" shows the import of these film-makers' "armed eye" (1989: 20). For Virilio, what this movement points to is nothing less than the fact that such film-makers "were themselves merely being hijacked by war." That's why, for these battle-hardened warriors, the fusion of war, weaponry, and the human eye amounted to a sort of logistics wherein "they thought that, like airmen, they formed part of a kind of technical elite." This "final privilege of their art" not only showed the film-makers a "military technology in action," but also demonstrated to them how to serve up to the public such capacities for movement as innovative technological special effects and spectacles, or what he calls the "continuation of the war's destruction of form."

What is critical for Virilio's explanation is that cinema and aerialized war are thought of as interdependent, but not portrayed as a seductive modern technical beyond. All that can be deduced is that there is continual escalation. He elucidates this by way of his discussion of "air reconnaissance operations for the US expeditionary corps during the First World War," which produced so much war information in the form of photographic prints that the "photograph ceased to be an episodic item" (pp. 20–1). From World War I onwards, then, the photograph turned into "a veritable *flow of pictures* which fitted perfectly with the statistical tendencies of this first great military-industrial conflict" (p. 21; my emphasis). Yet Virilio's description of photo-cum-cinematic escalation repudiates the setting up of a model for cinematic or military development from which an "end of cinema and/ or war" argument can be inferred, and it questions any single viewpoint or method for contending with cinematic or military events. All we are left with is the understanding that there is photo-cum-cinematic escalation, that war is central to it, and that the ongoing militarization of aesthetics must be countered. This is not Baudrillard's cinema and the aesthetics of disappearance, and it is considerably more substantial than his idea of a postmodern philosophy of cinema and technology, reality and history.

Thus Virilio's description of the relation between war, weaponry, and the human eye, of the logistics of perception, necessitates responses from critics of the military without pre-establishing what form those responses must take. One line of response or critique concerning the logistics of perception might be a focus on the "general interpretation mania" depicted in "Cinema Isn't I See, It's I Fly" (p. 21), a mania that is imposed by our sense of apartness from cinema as an indirect, non-logical form of perception. Virilio's concern with the logistics of perception is, then, primarily about escalation and about film-makers being hijacked by war. The logistics of perception therefore involves the escalation of militarized organizations and frameworks that represent themselves as global through the medium of cinema. In truth, such military perceptual logistics have become for Virilio the points at which the developmental and intensive ways of organizing cinema and aerialized war are no longer questioned. Rather, they have continued to evolve into new kinds of logistics of perception. One such recent innovation is of course the "logistic of electro-optic perception," which is represented by that "airplane without a pilot", the "aerial reconnaissance *drone*", which is "equipped with a simple video camera" (2002a: 107).

Yet cinema and aerialization during World War II and beyond, as a mélange of pictorialism and logistics, were and are deeply ambivalent cine-military systems. Even so, during World War II, for example, these systems' coded information and propaganda still managed to find their way into the pressurized cockpits of Allied bombers. Here, as later in the Gulf and Kosovo Wars, the logistics of perception need the bombers' cockpits to "become artificial synthesizers that shut out the world of the senses" (Virilio 1989: 24). But, throughout World War II at least, the results of military–technological separation were so acute and long term that Allied bomber command responded by lightening such feelings, associated as they were with "the dangerous passage of its armadas over Europe," by "painting brightly colored cartoon heroes or giant pin-ups with evocative names over the camouflage." "In a kind of CB system," Virilio writes, "honey-tongued female announcers not only assumed radio guidance of the crews but also helped them through their mission by blurring the image of destruction with jokes, personal confidences, and even songs of love." What he is emphasizing here in *War and Cinema*, as well as in *Desert Screen* and *Strategy of Deception*, is that the bombers' artificial synthesizers, required by what he has labeled the logistics of perception, identify new technical vectors of the beyond or new fusions of cinema with an inexhaustible variety of communications technologies and seductive human voices, every one of which allows different military technologies and aerial possibilities to appear. The logistics of perception are, then, seemingly humanity's current "mission," which involves not only picnolepsy but also the blurring and, ultimately, the explosion of the image that the female announcers' funny stories, intimate secrets, and love songs sought to prevent. Thus the logistics of perception is also a kind of historical and contemporary sensation that demands the escalated, yet accurate reproduction of audiovisual effects. The capacities for movement that are themselves the foundation of the logistics of perception are used to "soften" our exposure to nuclear and other explosions, but the logistics of perception represents the truth of their existence, for example by means of Stanley Kubrick's precise duplication of such audiovisual effects "when he used Vera Lynn singing of 'We'll Meet Again' to soften the long series of nuclear explosions that conclude *Dr Strangelove*." The work of the critic of the art

WILEY

wiley.com

Title: VIRILIO MEDIA

Author: ARMITAGE

ISBN: 9780745642291

Price: 19.95

Media Contact:
MARIANNE RUTTER

Phone: 781-388-8529

Email:
MRUTTER@WILEY.COM

For more information on this book and other news from Wiley, please visit our press room at www.wiley.com/go/press

of technology is therefore to try to interpret these logistics of perception much as we might try to understand a film like *Dr Strangelove*, which everyone has seen many times before. There are no predetermined laws for these readings that spell out their implications beforehand, and no explanation is ever conclusive. Alternatively, explications should constantly be inspired by and receptive to a sharp awareness of reality, and they should go directly to the increasingly uniform core of the ever proliferating war image, recognizing that, after the logistics of perception, "nothing is left but the recording of successive states of discharged matter."

CONCLUSION

Virilio argues that the age of the aesthetics of disappearance is one in which global cinema in effect became weaponized. He maintains that there are particular capacities for movement, whose influence on specific ideas of global escalation makes them constitute a logistics of perception or of the escalation of the modern technical beyond. In *War and Cinema*, *Desert Screen*, and *Strategy of Deception*, the key example of this phenomenon is cinema. Here, he claims, the modern technical beyond of "flying into the unknown" escalates because of the fatal interdependence of cinema and war. However, this and other logistics of perception are open to more than mere narratives of the aggressive colors of American films. Rather, they necessitate responses from across a variety of disciplines, for example to issues of nationalism and, crucially, to the question of whether military and cinematic victories in wartime have now become one.

In opposition to other media theorists such as Jean Baudrillard, who advocates a turn to a postmodern account of cinematic images and war and whose writings present the aesthetics of disappearance as a primeval pleasure, Virilio insists on the importance of examining the logistics of perception. He argues that cinema, and especially aerialized war, should be thought of through the idea of escalation, since the contemporary logistics of perception points to the increasing uniformity of cinematic and military systems, and it is this homogeneity that offers the focal point for the critic of the art of cinematic technologies.

3

NEW MEDIA

Vision, Inertia, and the Mobile Phone

INTRODUCTION

In his later work Virilio maintains the idea of the importance of interrogating the suppositions of cinema and war considered in Chapter 2. However, his focus is on the far-reaching technological capability of the logistics of perception, or the theoretical category he names "the vision machine" (Virilio 1994b).

The vision machine has two meanings in Virilio's philosophy. The restricted meaning is the examination of vision technologies. More commonly, it indicates the entire process of the production and dissemination of images throughout history, which Virilio retraces by way of aesthetics, military technologies, and urban planning in the era of virtual reality – a "reality" that he radically redefines as rooted in a new, "paradoxical logic" of the image. The vision machine as a specific subject of investigation emerged in his writings during the 1980s, alongside his work on the philosophy of painting, engraving, and architecture. Ever since, it has formed an important part of his discussion of numerous philosophers dealt with in his books, chiefly Maurice Merleau-Ponty (1968) and Gilles Deleuze (2001; 2005). In debates over modern and postmodern technologies of perception, he uses the vision machine both in the limited sense of a philosophy of vision technologies and in the more wide-ranging sense of a historical account of the manufacture and distribution of images.

In another book, entitled *Polar Inertia* (2000a), Virilio concentrates his attention on the possibilities of this concept, its condition, and its associated visual regime to contest recognized beliefs about the relationship between space, time, and technology. What makes this book vital for appreciating Virilio's theory of new media technologies is that its focus on the "here and now" of vision, space, territory, and the body produces an explanation of polar inertia that is more finely wrought and multifaceted than that expounded in any of his other main writings such as *The Aesthetics of Disappearance*. This chapter will explain the case that Virilio makes in *Polar Inertia*; it will distinguish clearly the important stages in his thoughts on its globalization; and it will present his concept of the mobile phone that works by means of a cellular radio system, a form of "universal remote control," as he discusses it in *The University of Disaster* (2010a) and revisits continually in his latest texts (see Virilio and Armitage 2009; Virilio 2010b; 2012). But, first, it is helpful to provide the background to Virilio's deployment of the concept of polar inertia by looking at the main contentions of that book.

If *The Aesthetics of Disappearance* describes the condition of picnolepsy, photography, and film in relation to postmodern technical prostheses, *Polar Inertia* reflects on the "place" and value of vision and stasis in postmodern culture. Virilio claims that we have entered the age of polar inertia, as notions of here and now, space, place, and stopping points,

NEW MEDIA: VISION, INERTIA, AND THE MOBILE PHONE   73

not to mention movement, have all undergone a shift "from the earth as centre (the axis of reference for the Ancients)" to our "*living present* as centre" (2000a: 71).

Virilio's conception of polar inertia derives from his stance on contemporary philosophy; this notion signifies the "basic fixation" of "*the world as proto-foundation of meaning*" (2000a: 71). As an experimental philosopher, he developed the idea of polar inertia late in the twentieth century, to describe his own standpoint concerning a sociocultural condition that, for him, is "not so much original as terminal." For Virilio, the moon landing of July 21, 1969 was world-shattering in the sense that it engendered and imparted novel concepts and potentialities for human civilization. As a typically French philosopher and critic of the art of technology, he has written a kind of manifesto that clarifies the nature, development, and implications of polar inertia, which causes "the reference ground [*sol*] to lose its importance and to become an *entresol*" (p. 72). The archetypal character, development, and repercussions of polar inertia are encapsulated in Virilio's declaration that the "effort to develop [. . .] rockets [. . .] ended in liquidation of the ground of reference, when the *axis mundi* lost forever its absolute value." It is this conception of the "liquidation of the ground of reference," in addition to the sense of destroying well-known ideas about the world of "absolute value," that Virilio takes hold of and examines in his work on polar inertia.

From his earliest writings, Virilio has been a critic of polar inertia, especially regarding vision (see, for instance, his work on television and the remote control (1997), the Kosovo War (2000b), or inertial guidance systems (2005a)). Indeed, his discussion of polar inertia is rooted in a critique of our destruction of the skies, of the landing of humans on remote planets, and of the envisioning of a void that is the outer limit of the stars.

While *Polar Inertia* catalogs a succession of criticisms unleashed by Virilio against wiping out the heavens, I want to concentrate initially on his examination of modern and postmodern vision technologies in *The Vision Machine*. His resistance to objects perceiving us is then introduced in this chapter. *The Vision Machine* is thus worth expounding here because the differences between his arguments in this text and those presented in *Polar Inertia* make it simpler to grasp both the perspective he adopts and the alternatives he proposes – namely limited human vision and unlimited technological vision in relation to machines.

In *The Vision Machine* Virilio outlines his critique of the ability of vision machines "not only of recognizing the contours of shapes, but also of completely interpreting the visual field" (1994b: 59); and his study of their relation to complex environments, close-ups, and distance is poles apart from that of other contemporary philosophers. His critical focus on the new media technology of "visionics" does not express merely an obscure or theoretical consideration of the nature of polar inertia or vision, or even a postmodern argument about whether vision machines are good or evil. Instead, for Virilio, visionics has the potential to produce *"sightless vision"* and to reveal the dehumanizing influence of video cameras controlled by computers. His notions of the place of vision thus hinge on particular suppositions concerning computers and vision machines, and they offer a distinct form of new media theory about ambient environments, objects, and the prospect of a fully automated culture.

THE VISION MACHINE

Virilio (1994b: 59) argues that, under the influence of contemporary technology, the ability of "televiewers" to analyze or interpret the meaning of events has become industrialized, by which he implies that developments in production, stock control, and military robotics are cherished for their preparation of the way for the accelerated "*automation of perception*" sooner than their potential to enhance human vision. Or, to put it differently, innovations in artificial vision have become ends in themselves and pay little heed to the escalated effect they have on mass individualism and its visual capacities. The outcome of this, he says, is that "delegating the analysis of objective reality" to vision machines makes it imperative to consider "the nature of the virtual image," and that this "formation of optical imagery with no apparent base, with no permanency beyond that of mental or instrumental visual memory" significantly affects our entire way of life by organizing the audiovisual logics that shape postmodern culture.

Virilio argues that we should resist this virtualization of visual cultural life and that this can best be accomplished through the idea of "blindness" as a way of revealing the diverse vision technologies that structure contemporary culture (pp. 72–3). It is in this sense that, for Virilio, modern and postmodern vision technologies increasingly involve the production of "sightless vision" (p. 73). His vision machine is thus "merely the reproduction of an intense blindness that will become the latest and last form of industrialization: *the industrialization of the non-gaze*," and we must continue to resist it. Accordingly, he elaborates a hypothesis concerning paradoxical logic, a technocratic idea that, following "the invention of video recording, holography, and computer graphics," implies that the twenty-first century is "marked by the end of a logic of public representation" (p. 63). His aim, therefore, is to alert us to the fact that "we still cannot seem to get a grip on the *virtualities* of the paradoxical logic of the videogram, the hologram, or digital imagery." For Virilio, "this probably explains the frantic 'interpretosis' that still surrounds these technologies today in the press, as well as the proliferation and instant obsolescence of different computer and audiovisual equipment." He argues that *"paradoxical logic* emerges when the real-time image dominates the thing represented," and that the aim of his new media theory is to establish the conditions under which the paradoxical logic of real time and virtual space do not prevail over human time and actual space.

The Vision Machine is a contentious book, which closes with an assault on vision technologies, automated perception included: according to Virilio, they threaten our recognition and interpretation of the postmodern visual field. He understands these vision technologies as generating a "crisis of perceptive faith" (p. 75): as technologies that have severed the connection between seeing and the contemporary human body. One of the main areas of the crisis of perceptive faith that he condemns is the rise of a technologized vision. Technologized vision, he maintains, should be considered as part of the wider project of video optics, of digital or image blindness, and its task of encumbering us to understand or see the world about us ought to be recaptured from these technologized facilitators of recognition and shapes whose synthetic images and vision are essentially unintelligible to us because we do not share their ability to produce "statistical imagery."

For Virilio, the statistical image is the epitome of blind technologized vision. He argues that the end of the twentieth century witnessed the emergence of the statistical image "thanks to rapid calculation of the pixels a computer graphics system can display on a screen" (ibid.). Such "decoded" individual pixels not only destroy human vision but also offer new kinds of blindness, by forming new relations with the pixels immediately surrounding them, to redefine postmodern culture. Furthermore, Virilio reasons that the contemporary statistical image has conquered all others and has succeeded despite the crisis of perceptive faith (of which polar inertia is one major feature), since it is currently inflicting a new sort of analysis, statistical thought, on visual culture and on society more generally. With this perspective on the condition of vision technologies to hand, Virilio explains what he understands their possible effect to be in terms of their capacity to produce "rational illusions" or a digitized "statistical optics" able to influence destructively our visual comprehension and our ways of theorizing new media. What he means by this is that statistical thought, when it is ensnared within the technologized facilitator of recognition that is the vision machine, within the sphere of synthetic images or vision, becomes a means by which we can no longer perceive rationally our real visual position or enunciate our actual visual desires. What is significant about the computer, then, is not its digital optics per se, but the way we put to use specific vision machines and forms of statistical optics to acquire a diminished knowledge of our visual position and an enhanced opportunity to fool ourselves with rational illusions.

Possibly the simplest example of this procedure involving the appropriation of statistical thought to illuminate contemporary cultural life can be discovered in a "fable based on a very real invention" (p. 76). In *The Vision Machine*, for instance, Virilio discusses the *"calculator pen"* to describe the act of contemporary writing:

All you have to do is to write the computation on paper, as you would if you were doing the sum yourself. When you finish writing, the little screen built into the pen displays the result. Magic? No way. While you are writing, an optical system *reads* the numbers formed and the electronic component does the sum. (Ibid.)

In this example it is unimportant whether one pays attention to the facts or not; what is significant about the tale is what the pen, "a blind pen this time, will write down for you, the reader, as the final words of this book" (ibid.). He continues:

> Imagine for a moment that to write the book I have borrowed technology's state-of-the-art pen: the *reader pen*. What do you think will come up on the screen, abuse or praise? Only, have you ever heard of a writer who only writes for his pen [. . .]?

For Virilio, this is the aim of vision machines: to visualize and technologize all the possibilities of paradoxical logic and to establish a space where ideas of computerized recording and graphics can be escalated and extended.

POLAR INERTIA: THE IMPACT OF THE MOON LANDING

In his reaction to the advent of the vision machine, to the production of sightless vision, Virilio argues that it is impossible to "talk about the development of the audiovisual without also talking about the development of virtual imagery and its influence on human behavior, or without pointing to the new *industrialization of vision*, to the growth of a veritable market in synthetic perception" (1994b: 59), thus opening the way for a discussion of "all the ethical questions this entails." To all intents and purposes, in *The Vision Machine* he endeavors to reveal the "essence" of vision technologies involving virtual images, the industrialization of vision, and artificial perception through the study of the vision machine's paradoxical logic and in an approach that modern philosophers of technological "enframing," through their repeated exertions to do something similar over the course of the twentieth century, have demonstrated to be practically impossible (see for example Heidegger 1978: 307–42 for what is arguably the most successful attempt). The complexity of this revelation is most obvious in Virilio's speculative writings on the contemporary philosophical aspects of the moon landing of July 21, 1969.

Certainly, in developing his ethical ideas beyond *The Vision Machine*, Virilio begins to question whether in fact vision technologies can ever reveal their own essence, or indeed whether the analysis of their paradoxical logic is a theoretical or practical possibility. However, such questions, he argues in *Polar Inertia*, can be reframed through a consideration of vision machines not with regard to their revelation of their own essence or paradoxical logic, but in relation to Apollo 11 landing on the moon (2000a: 72). As he contends, vision machines reveal a great deal not only about images, but also about the fact that, at the "precise moment" of the moon landing, "altitude had become 'distance,' pure and simple." For Virilio, therefore, the moon landing signifies that there is "now another ground or basis, *a ground up above*," and that today "looking at the moon" has become "the same as looking at an island from a shoreline." But he also claims that the price of this "looking" was the "obliteration of the sky" and the unexpected emergence of a "balcony view of the void" where "the outer limits suddenly became a starry coast." Here he links the idea of the void, of the outer limits, of "disappropriation," with the "celestial object called earth" that "was henceforth of less interest than the time and space separating the two heavenly bodies." Nevertheless, what is important to remember here concerning these shifts in the nature of looking, of the sky, and of the void is that, for him, vision machines also reveal another kind of outer limit, which is the outer limit of a science that has "become so technical" that philosophers are now "incapable of understanding it" (p. 73).

Rather than discussing vision machines in relation to the revelation of their essence and paradoxical logic, then, Virilio now emphasizes the landing on the moon, along with Auschwitz, Hiroshima, and Nagasaki, as part of the "fall-out" from an increasingly universal technoscience without consciousness or conscience (p. 74). He examines the potential that vision machines have to reveal that, once "lunar soil has been reached," our world suffers a "loss of extension" that "brings with it the decline of that constituted world-time" he understands as being identical with human psychological time. Indeed, the point about vision machines becomes for him one concerning their ability to dislocate our relationship with the constitutive time and space of human psychology.

In *Polar Inertia* and elsewhere (Virilio 1995: 133–56; 1997: 9–21; 2010a: 51–74), Virilio distinguishes three kinds of visual and technocultural sites: universal remote control space, statistical imagery, and polar inertia. In other debates related to polar inertia, comparable ideas map a historical route of visual and socio-technological development. For instance, Deleuze asserts that today "we're at the beginning of something new," namely, in the prison system, "the attempt to find 'alternatives' to custody, at least for minor offenses, and the use of electronic tagging to force offenders to stay at home between certain hours" (Deleuze 1995: 182). In Deleuze's methodology, universal remote control space is depicted as the most important social form of the late twentieth century, and it is to be discovered in the literary works of writers such as William Burroughs (1968). Statistical imagery like code and password, information, sample, and data is, similarly, a key element of universal remote control space for Deleuze. Polar inertia is, then, a recent visual and socio-technological development; it expands the assumptions of statistical imagery and, as we know, it is to be found primarily in the writings of Virilio, who, as Deleuze puts it, has, for some considerable time, been "analyzing the ultrarapid forms of apparently free-floating control that are taking over from the old disciplines at work within the timescales of closed systems" (Deleuze 1995: 178).

Although Deleuze's method of differentiating between the three kinds of visual and technocultural sites is useful in the case of the prison system and so forth, this is not the distinction that Virilio sets up in *Polar Inertia*. In its place he offers a more complex image of vision and technoculture, where universal remote control space, statistical imagery, and polar inertia coexist in the present period of visual and technological production. Accordingly, in contrast to Virilio's *Aesthetics of Disappearance*, which explains the polar inertia of Howard Hughes as a corpse-like fixity in the Desert Inn in Las Vegas, *Polar Inertia* is concerned with the impact that vision technologies have on our sense of movement. Virilio argues that contemporary vision machines are driven by statistical imagery, which then becomes a key element of polar inertia. Thus understood, polar inertia is not the same thing as statistical imagery, but a consequence of it, and at present this effect is being relentlessly escalated and expanded throughout contemporary culture and society. Polar inertia therefore does not come into view in its full form under the modernity of the twentieth century. Rather, it is inexorably dispersing itself within the "hypermodernity" (Lipovetsky 2005) of the twenty-first century. In short, the coming of the age of polar inertia is in large part the result of the transformations wrought by statistical imagery. According to Virilio, statistical imagery is thus in a condition of endless disturbance and development owing to its incessant efforts to "improve" and "progress." For him, polar inertia is an almost military power within the confusions of this hypermodernity that confronts

and destroys existing visual ideas and technological categories (Virilio 2010a: 51–74). Moreover, it makes possible the
emergence of novel yet wholly destructive modes of thought
and sightless vision, which only reveal still further those
dominant hypermodern themes of "continuous improvement," or what he calls the "propaganda of progress" (Virilio
and Armitage 2009: 107).

THE MOBILE PHONE: UNIVERSAL REMOTE
CONTROL

Along these lines, Virilio portrays as polar inertia our "sightless" visual activities on our mobile phones, for instance,
where we "now not only see the same thing at the same
time" but also "inter-react" with real time communications
and information, which resembles "an emotional 'fusion'" of
"interlocutors," of "being carried away" by a "reflex action"
(2010a: 7). Zeroing in on how, despite their name, "mobile
phones that can do anything, hear anything, see anything"
actually destroy the ideas of movement and transport that
were present in Europe and the United States from the
beginning of the modern period, Virilio (pp. 45, 81) argues
that, as with the Internet, the mobile phone invites "all the
dangers of the outside world" not merely inside, "into each
and everyone's home," but also into "the palm of their hand"
by way of video teleconferencing and so on. Indeed, for him,
"the development of the mobile phone" is actually the pre-
cursor of the wearing of "intelligent garments, those future
'electronic straightjackets'" that herald a "universal remote
control" (p. 88). "In such a remote-controlled existence,"
writes Virilio,

> the individual will be kept in constant contact, at every
> moment and at every point in their trajectory, so that they

will no longer be left with any spare time [. . .] for prolonged introspection. For tomorrow we will all be monopolized by the growing outsourcing of our once immediate sensations; we will all suddenly be collectivized in our affects, in our most intimate emotions, slipping and sliding or, more precisely, "surfing" as we will then be in a new sort of epidemic of cooperation; the pandemic of a mob once solitary, now plagued with the delirium of a UNANIMISM that the prophets of doom of the twentieth century foretold. (Ibid.)

Actually, Virilio argues that his philosophy of the impact of the moon landing indicates the simultaneous introduction of the hypermodern "DROMOMANIAC" and of the "deserter of the environment" (p. 97). And, like the hypermodern dromomaniacs and the deserters of the environment, the moon landing is also an introduction to hypermodernity's speed addictions – by which Virilio means that it stands at the beginning of hypermodernity's unsuspecting participation in the "great mutation in planetary settlement whereby the sedentary man is now everywhere at home thanks to his mobile – in the TGV [*train à grade vitesse*], in the supersonic jet as in his place of residence – and the nomad is nowhere at home"; and this at the same time initiates the theme of the pedestrian who uses the mobile phone and is thereby "straying off-course, at the risk of in turn causing accidents related to his 'passing locomobility,' and so, behaving like someone in a state of drunkenness," and who will bring it about, "unwittingly," that "the ordinary passerby" becomes an "involuntary choreographer of a handicap which certain nervous diseases are a patent sign of." "Not content to eliminate anything to the side of his path from his field of vision," Virilio writes, "the contemporary pedestrian of cellular videophony is so busy concentrating on the audiovisible interlocutor he's calling, he scarcely sees in front of his nose":

Faced with the improbable success of such telephone practices, surely we've worked out that this new "body technology" will soon give rise [. . .] to enthusiastic celebration of this kind of postural drift and the disjointed, unbalanced style of walking that goes with it [. . .]

So, making himself unfamiliar with the immediate area lining his walk [. . .] the solitary pedestrian will perhaps, one day, wind up completely neglecting the life around him, so close to hand as he rambles along, and become instead completely engrossed in the collective imagination of an audiovisible "far-away land" that will satisfy his expectations to the detriment of any actual encounter. (2010a: 98)

Virilio's idea of the overlapping of mobile phones with polar inertia within the city is complicated, and to explain it I will now consider in depth his characterizations of universal remote control space, statistical imagery, and polar inertia.

ON THE ORIGINS OF UNIVERSAL REMOTE CONTROL SPACE

For Virilio, universal remote control space involves "the progressive disappearance of the space of anthropological–geographic reference in favor of a culture of a mere *visual piloting*" (2000a: 76). It is the visual technoculture of the ceaseless "'transfers of responsibility' that will soon have created a new horizon of human experience." He maintains, quoting Werner von Braun: "Tomorrow, to learn space will be as useful as learning to drive a car." This "corrects" the generally accepted theoretical viewpoint on space. In place of the "full space" of the "primal ark," he claims that an ever increasing control makes the Earth seem to be "the *empty space* of an extra-terrestrial vessel." What he is arguing here is that this "final ark" is "coming to replace the 'space–time' of our ordinary experience of place with that of the non-place" of contemporary visual culture, of the "space-speed" of technoculture, and that "speed really is the 'transfer accident,' the premature ageing of the constituted world." This is why *Polar Inertia* contends that, carried away by the "extreme violence" of speed, postmodern visual culture does "not go anywhere; it merely abandons the *living* in favor of the *void* and of rapidity," and thus we do little except watch our computer and mobile phone screens and monitor our own "interactive trajectory." For him, this is a "journey" with no visual distance, "a 'travelling time' with no actual passing of time." It portrays the world to us in a way that is simply a matter of "organizing the real-time conductivity of images and information." Tomorrow, therefore, by way of watching our screens and monitoring our interactive trajectory, our "environmental control" will help to achieve an absolute speed, or a "dromo-politics" where "the nation will give way to social deregulation and transpolitical deconstruction." Here the newly established vision technologies such as mobile phones are presented as false or unnatural and exposed to critique with the intention of making us resist their influence.

This universal remote control space "will gradually replace not only direct command but above all ethics" in many fields, including genetics, ecology, and economics (p. 77). Nevertheless, this is not the full extent of Virilio's description: many of the vision machines that are usually depicted as being related to polar inertia by other theorists are also classified as being linked to universal remote control space in *Polar Inertia*. Virilio is keen to differentiate his own explanation of polar inertia from, for example, Deleuze's account of it, which states that polar inertia is a consequence of the statistical imagery of vision technologies and is anchored both in information and in what Virilio calls the idea of "omnipresence" (p. 78). For Virilio, the concept of omni-presence does not capture the entirety of polar inertia; rather it is the universal remote control space of our animal body. In this situation of accelerated information, circulation, and universal cultural remote control, space becomes radical and subversive; indeed, universal remote control space becomes a function of our animal body. Virilio maintains that this is increasingly the everyday experience of postmodern cultural exchange: the entire world of information increases and becomes total. It is thus universal remote control space that becomes omnipresent. Certainly, we increasingly accept universal remote control space as a stand-in for our natural world, our only real location, as the vision technologies of our contemporary culture continue to proliferate across postmodern society and declare their control over our animal bodies. The instability of the world is then replaced by the "stability" of vision technologies that, universally and remotely, control today's culture and its inhabitants from within themselves.

STATISTICAL IMAGERY, POLAR INERTIA, AND THE ACCIDENT: THE GRADUAL SPREAD OF A SOCIOPOLITICAL CYBERNETICS

In attempting to combat ever faster information circulation in the era of universal remote control space, Virilio offers two root causes of the problem – statistical imagery and polar inertia – both of which, if left unchecked, will destroy universal remote control space by way of the "implosion of real time" that "now conditions all exchanges" (2000a: 78). These are not two completely dissimilar computer-driven or catastrophic forms. More readily, polar inertia is the outcome of statistical imagery and it further exacerbates the latter's challenges to the very possibility of universal remote control space. Elsewhere Virilio argues that World War II was "the main catalyst in the development of a purely statistical notion of INFORMATION due to the strategic necessities of intelligence" (1995: 135), and that this led to "the gradual spread of a SOCIOPOLITICAL CYBERNETICS that tends to eliminate not only the weak, but also the component of free-will in human work, promoting [. . .] so-called 'interactive user-friendliness.'" The idea of the spread of sociopolitical cybernetics is important in his consideration of vision technologies, but it has almost totally been overlooked. Since it is so central for his argument concerning statistical imagery and polar inertia, it is vital to understand what might be at issue in it. Virilio develops his concept of the spread of sociopolitical cybernetics alongside his own discussion of the accident.

His philosophy of the accident stems from Aristotle (1998: 150). However, during the twentieth and twenty-first centuries, with the growth of vision machines, the accident has become a topic of discussion and argument. For Virilio, the central elements and portents of the accident are to be found in the postmodern theoretical features of the moon landing. In *Polar Inertia* he differentiates between two forms of visual and spatiotemporal, accelerated, and technoscientific experience: the "accident of accidents" and the "transfer accident" (2000a: 75–6). Both of these are events that happen when one comes in contact with the birth of a specific time (whether it is a desire, an observation, a live event, or the production of a primal time). The accident of accidents is an event, an absolute singularity, which is another name for the birth of time itself: "This ubiquitous desire to observe – to *see live*, why not? – the production of a primal time expresses," says Virilio, "better than any philosophical discourse on the 'invention' of time the will to power of universal science" (p. 75). With the transfer accident, events are perhaps more complicated. For here one is simultaneously carried away by the extreme violence of speed and aware that one does not go anywhere following the birth of this specific time: "we merely abandon the *living* in favor of the *void* of rapidity" (p. 76).

For Virilio (p. 78), the events of the transfer accident occur when, for example, one confronts the cybernetic program trading or automatic quoting of stock values in the City of London and Wall Street, which was commonly referred to in the 1980s as the "Big Bang" and which triggered the advent of the global economy. Virilio argues that our continued faith in program trading and similar cybernetic structures is mistaken, given the implosion of such real-time systems on Black Monday (October 19, 1987) and on May 6, 2010 when the "flash crash" or stock market crash of American corporate stocks was followed by a near instantaneous bounce back (Crosthwaite 2011: 177–99). Moreover, the implosion of such real-time systems "now conditions all exchanges, and the computer-driven crashes of 1987 [and 2010] were but an advance sign of other economic catastrophes" to come (Virilio 2000a: 78). In this sense, the implosion of such real-time systems designates through its eventhood that our largely unacknowledged dependence on "clever" appliances leads increasingly to a series of "dramatic breaks in the field of trade and social communication." What brings about the event of the transfer accident is, then, the spread of sociopolitical cybernetics; but within that event it is possible to imagine that the quicker information flows, "the more the control of all exchange increases and tends to become absolute." Hence, Virilio's conception of the transfer accident is derived from his idea of the spread of sociopolitical cybernetics.

Virilio has invented the concept of the transfer accident to explain how contemporary vision machines, from computers to mobile phones, can destroy even other, more established vision technologies, as well as substitute themselves for our natural environment. The statistical imagery of vision machines, he argues, has the ability slowly but surely to extend sociopolitical cybernetics, in other words to eradicate the element of autonomy in human labor and to advance a supposed "interactive user-friendliness."

Following the events of the transfer accident (their implosion of real-time systems, their conditioning of all exchanges, and their function as warning signs), the existing spread of sociopolitical cybernetics can be indicated by the transfer accident in two separate ways, one of which Virilio labels "statistical imagery" and the other "polar inertia." This distinction is at the root of the difference between the two forms, and he portrays it in terms of the "innovatory role of statistics" and its imagery "in fine-tuning the theory of *cybernetic domination*" (1995: 136) and the increasing "fragility of human 'self-consciousness'" concerning polar inertia (2000a: 78). The transfer accident of statistical imagery is thus engaged with events associated with cybernetic domination: the old vision technologies of, say, analog photography and cinema no longer represent the world sufficiently, and the events induced are increasingly militarized; following Norbert Wiener, Virilio warns us about the impending dangers of "the MILITARY–COMMUNICATIONS COMPLEX" (1995: 136). Conversely, the transfer accident of polar inertia acts through a sense of dread at the possible stasis or breakdown of vision technologies: the new logics of movement might grind to a halt and thus generate widespread fear of the new forms of temporality and immobility. For Virilio, such foreboding thus "reveals the hypertension of people living today," as everybody "can easily imagine the standstill" or the collapsing structure of universal remote control space, which will surely affect and challenge vision machines one day, and which itself points to the possibility of a new "behavioral inertia due to speed and the reduced depth of field of their [increasingly 'infirm'] immediate activities," as well as to multiply handicapped ways of experiencing and thinking about the mediated world (2000a: 78). Are we not, for example, already witnessing, daily, the face-to-face mobile phone-induced crashes of those "clever" and "cool," yet somehow also isolated individuals who are "OBJECT-oriented" but "SUBJECT-disoriented" (p. 98)?

Usefully, Virilio supplies a lucid illustration of the difference between statistical imagery and polar inertia, each of which, he claims, refers to the ongoing proliferation of sociopolitical cybernetics. On the side of statistical imagery, and following Karl Popper (1990), he puts statistical tendencies, which, according to Virilio's thesis, "people often take for facts, so much so that they become a force in their own right, which we then have to reckon with" (1995: 148). His hypotheses regarding statistical tendencies (p. 150) are, then, a generalization concerning the idea of statistics as a dynamic force; certainly in his conception our seemingly transparent universe is in fact "the product of a hidden motor," the statistical imagery of vision machines. The *"present time"* of vision machines can thus only correctly be described today as the "discrete advent of a *real time* that is itself nothing more than the outcome of a sort of general statistics of historical evolution," our present "reality" only ever being a synthetic illusion. Consequently, according to him, cyberspace, for example, as our "living present," is "hardly more than a "LIVING CINEMA" (p. 151). In short, "the transmission revolution" is now gearing up to expand sociopolitical cybernetics by way of a motorization of all metropolitan and cultural space. Mobile phones, for instance, contribute to a cyberspatial "urban displacement" that renders our everyday life increasingly "uninhabitable" as human physical movement becomes cinematic, becomes a kind of high-tech "'obstacle race' in which the other person ceases to be anything more than an adversary, at best a competitor," and "one you only encounter once" (Virilio 2010a: 98). Hence, thanks to the mushrooming of mobile phones and of the sociopolitical "digital imagery of the computer motor," "perceptual faith" is "letting itself be abused [. . .] by the virtuality generator." For Virilio, this makes statistical imagery and its tendencies a form of cybernetic domination: it allows the spread of sociopolitical cybernetics to be invoked as the dynamized artifice of calculating speed, while "the *real-space perspective* of the painters of the Quattrocento," because of the "computer cognoscenti of the Novocento," continues to be replaced by the perspective of real time.

In contrast to this situation, Virilio (1997: 9–21; 2000a: 82–6; 2010a: 57–64) raises the question of instantaneous "teleaction" as polar inertia. He argues that teleaction "raises once again the philosophical and political problems traditionally associated with the notions of *atopia* and *utopia*" (1997: 10) and further promotes not only the spread of sociopolitical cybernetics, but also "what is already being referred to as *teletopia*, with all the numerous paradoxes attendant on this." He employs a whole range of oxymorons (such as "meeting at a distance") and of contradictory questions concerning "being telepresent." Indeed, he notes that today's "technophiliacs" appear to have little concern for the fact that the "teletechnologies of real time are [. . .] killing 'present' time by isolating it from its here and now," as experiments are performed with a "commutative elsewhere that no longer has anything to do with our 'concrete presence' in the world, but is the elsewhere of a 'discrete telepresence' that remains a complete mystery" (pp. 10–11). The transfer accident of teleaction is then not only an issue of the dynamized artifice of calculating speed, such as the perspective of real time, but also one of "being telepresent, here and elsewhere, *at the same time*" (p. 10). Virilio's use of concepts such as "real time," "real space–time," or "events," and his critique of the destructive tendencies of recognized and newly minted notions of place and cyberspace, challenge our assumptions about what a place is supposed to be and repeatedly undercut our now everyday longing to enter cyberspace, the "noplace of teletopical techniques." For, according to him, we are at present continually confused about our sense of the "place" of the "man–machine interface," even if that confusion at times appears as the fascinating sensory environment and invigorating technoscape that is the Internet or the mobile phone screen. Yet, he hopes, this very same technoscape may also, one day, guide us to broach critical questions concerning our daily spatio-temporal and technological activities.

Virilio's deliberation on "teleaction" leads to one of his most transparent explanations of the polar inertia associated with vision machines:

> the current revolution in transmission leads [. . .] to the innovation of the ultimate vehicle: the static audiovisual vehicle, marking the advent of a behavioral inertia in the sender/receiver that moves us along from the celebrated *retinal persistence* which permits the optical illusion of cinematic projection to the *bodily persistence* of this "terminal-man." (1997: 11)

For Virilio then, the polar inertia associated with the vision machines of the current transmission revolution destroys conventional audiovisual vehicles and vision technologies through the spread of sociopolitical cybernetics, not simply as the dynamized artifice of calculating speed but as statistical tendencies and images, or as a force that destroys customary ways of movement or behavior. The polar inertia of vision machines is the bodily persistence of "terminal-man": it smashes the logics and weakens the categories that the sender/receiver is accustomed to, and reintroduces questions such as "What is technologized vision?" and "What is an optical illusion?"

Therefore, for the Virilio of *Polar Inertia* and beyond – unlike for the Virilio of *The Vision Machine*, who sought to reveal the essence of vision technologies – it is vision technologies' ability to confuse, destroy, and challenge our assumptions about movement that is the source of their significance. The polar inertia of contemporary computers and mobile phones, he argues, tends to obliterate all efforts to refocus the ethics of animate being. This power to confront even long-established analog vision technologies gives digital vision machines a major role in Virilio's recent thought because he is fundamentally opposed to the spread of sociopolitical cybernetics.

CONCLUSION

Virilio's *Vision Machine* questions the role of new media vision technologies in the present period. In *Polar Inertia* he investigates the significance of the moon landing and of the transfer accident in terms of the potential they have to destroy traditional ways of seeing, as well as analog vision technologies. Since the transfer accident is symptomatic of the gradual spread of a sociopolitical cybernetics by means of contemporary digital vision technologies, it can pinpoint new possibilities for the critique of such destructive thoughts and actions. Unlike the Virilio of *The Vision Machine*, who argued that the purpose of studying vision technologies was that they had the capability to reveal their own essence, the Virilio of *Polar Inertia* and *The University of Disaster* sees vision technologies' function as devastating our everyday awareness of human movement – as we saw in the example of the mobile phone, which, for Virilio, is a form of universal remote control. What is important about these contentions of Virilio's, I have suggested, is that they alert us to the fact that the universal remote control space of vision technologies serves to obliterate our daily consciousness of motion. Furthermore, statistical imagery and polar inertia, through computers, mobile phones, and other vision technologies, cause the transfer accident, which merely reveals the outer limits of our knowledge and identifies new negative – as well as critical – horizons. For Virilio, polar inertia is but one crucial outcome of statistical imagery. In statistical imagery, he argues, the transfer accident emerges through the dynamized artifice of calculating speed, whereas the transfer accident of polar inertia annihilates our consciousness of being present in the here and now, of the constitutive time and space of human psychology.

4

CITY OF PANIC

The Instrumental Image Loop of Television and Media Events

INTRODUCTION

The purpose of this chapter is to consider Virilio's (2005b) conception of the "city of panic," which arises from his media theory. It does so through interpretations of four of Virilio's texts (2000c, 2002b, 2005b, 2007a), all of which continue many of the themes and concepts introduced in *The Aesthetics of Disappearance, War and Cinema, The Vision Machine*, and *Polar Inertia*, and by focusing on issues related to what I shall call "the instrumental image loop of television" and media events. The important question that steers this chapter is therefore: What kind of "landscape of events" (Virilio 2000c) or media theory is feasible, given the postmodern escalation of the modern technical beyond of "flying into the unknown"? In answering this question, the present chapter will summarize the arguments that Virilio (2005b) employs, and it will do so in order to ask media- and event-based questions about "the mutation of terrorism" and "theatrical militarism," "visual discourses of distraction" and the "synchronization of emotions," which will be contemplated in greater detail in the next four sections.

A LANDSCAPE OF EVENTS: THE MUTATION OF TERRORISM

In *A Landscape of Events* Virilio examines the mediated and urban connotations of his philosophy and describes what he sees as the role of television when one considers it with regard to the escalation of the modern technical beyond.

In "Delirious New York" Virilio offers one of his most unambiguous formulations about the relationships between events and the cityscape:

> The [1993] attack on the World Trade Center is the first of the post-Cold War. No matter who is responsible, it ushers in a new era of terrorism having nothing in common with the explosions that regularly rock Ireland or England. (2000c: 18)

Terror attacks are part of the landscape of events: they question the post-Cold War order and destroy the culture in which we live, while waging war on the status quo. Still, for Virilio, this questioning and destruction is linked to questions of television. He argues that televised media events entail, and emerge from, what he calls a "new era of terrorism" (ibid.). This is an era distinct from that of the "old era of terrorism." The old era of terrorism belonged in the age of nuclear deterrence and operated in the sphere or age of the balance of terror: it identified and described something similar to minor political crime; for instance, the "petty terrorism" of the age of nuclear deterrence indicated a situation that concerned "the traditional supremacy of 'weapons of destruction' [e.g. the atom bomb] and 'weapons of obstruction' [e.g. fortifications] – in other words, the duel of arms and armor" (p. 21). The new era of terrorism is part of a different form of attack: it does not merely change a situation but destroys it. Examples include the serious intention to bring down the World Trade Center in 1993, or the destruction of the Mumbai Stock Exchange on March 13, 1993. In both instances, there is no overt effort simply to transform how the world really is, but there is instead an effort to produce the required condition: total destruction. To put it differently, while the old era of terrorism attempted to transform the world, the new era of terrorism attempts to destroy it. For Virilio, this distinction between the old and the new eras of terrorism is the starting point for theorizing about media events, and especially about television.

Virilio argues that it is imperative to take account of the urban landscape when we consider the difference between the old and new eras of terrorism. In this he follows his own work, which, as this chapter argues, makes a connection between media events and the inner city, between strategic events and the shift in the military order. In his media theory, this relation is called "the mutation of terrorism" (Virilio 2000c: 18).

Indeed, Virilio claims that the kind of media- and event-based institution – for instance the United Nations (UN) – that disregards this mutation or confronts the new era of terrorism with the same convictions that re-established international tribunals and trials of the Cold War type (which, naturally, arise from the "authors of war crimes" themselves) can, if "terrorist practices" are not severely punished, bring about powerlessness and the imposition of "incredible damage not only on the innocent victims but also, and especially, on democracy" (p. 19). He argues that there are two ways in which postmodern media events can do this, and that these ways bear a resemblance to the escalation of the contemporary technical beyond of "flying into the unknown" delineated in *The Aesthetics of Disappearance*.

The first way of highlighting the difference between the new and the old era of terrorism is to center the former on the idea of the strategic event, after the manner of an escalation of the military order. This way transpires from the new era of war, which was inaugurated by the collapse of the Berlin Wall in 1989, and even to a greater extent by the Gulf War of 1990–1 (see Virilio 2002a). In this concept of media events, of a new era of war at the end of the age of the balance of terror, the age of collapsing walls and the reassertion of Western policies of war generate their own kinds of television from the frightening escalation of the uncertainties of American foreign policy. Television becomes part of the frightening escalation, and the notion of a Western policy of war that is developed involves particular types of catastrophe in the urban realm. This Western policy of war is a creation of the end of the age of the balance of terror – a creation that elaborates, in a string of new "security" statements, a theory of what will make life "safe." The landscape of events is then rooted in propositions such as: even if the Western policy of war causes uncertainty everywhere, nevertheless, the President of the United States (for example) should be given the capacity to implement it. The difficulty here is that the frightening escalation, and consequently television, are now driven by a military interventionism that decides for us how we must live, which is, preemptively, spawning a geopolitical system that remains beyond the recent resolutions of the UN Security Council. Examples include the Western policy that established the Gulf War on suppositions about its "humanitarian" dimensions, or military policies derived from a particular philosophy as in the Kosovo War of 1999, which had a specific view of what diplomacy and a thoroughly revived neocolonialism and military action could achieve. Yet, if Iraq's Saddam Hussein had no scruples during the Gulf and Iraq Wars and was prepared to use every sort of military means, "then tomorrow his UN adversaries will become like him" (Virilio 2002a: 81). Or, if the Kosovo War, as former British Prime Minister Tony Blair said, is a "new kind of war, about values as much as about territory," then he has "now ceased to attach importance to the physical conditions of a battle" (Virilio 2000b: 2). Hence this kind of Western policy of war is not only cruel and neocolonialist, but also immoral, totalizing, and contagious: the frightening escalation of the Western policy of war is given in advance, and people from Iraq and Kosovo to Britain and the United States begin conforming to its "military humanism" (Chomsky 1999) – in other words, to the transformation of everyday life into everyday war.

The second problematic form of strategic event related to the media, and to television in particular, connects more closely to terroristic escalation, to a kind of "flying into the unknown," or to what Virilio calls the *"age of imbalance"* (2000c: 19). In this formulation, television becomes associated with events such as the historic attack on the World Trade Center of 1993, which marks for Virilio the beginning of the most recent age of imbalance. In this paradigm, the new era of terrorism is not driven by a state's military interventionism as much as "inhabited" by the people of the great metropolises: for example, terrorist criminal acts shown on television escalate our fears, and therefore we are habituated to and come to have faith in, or at least accept, terrorized and fearful ways of life (Svendsen 2008). This is the foundation of an event-based paradigm of the Western policy of war, wherein we are expected to have an investment in that policy in so far as we associate ourselves with it, habituate ourselves to it, have trust in its preemptive ideals, support its future-oriented "anti-terrorist policies," and so on. But, Virilio maintains, this paradigm too can cause its own kind of helplessness, which is based on forms of mass media. As he argues, defenselessness is evident when Western policies of war come to dominate television, to offer constant representations of war, so that we are unable to reject or criticize, for instance, the meting out of inconceivable harm to ourselves and democracy brought about by the launch of the American Military Channel, which broadcasts "documentaries and serials about war, weapons, and explosives twenty-four hours a day!" (Virilio 2000c: 20). The association of television with the momentous assault on the World Trade Center of 1993 thus allows such significant assaults to become the launch pad for the further militarization of television. Certainly, those caught in the Western policy of war-making who do not hold its ideals or those of the Military Channel, perhaps on the basis of their conscientious objections, are simply not recognized by militarized television. We need only recall the numerous broadcast documentaries on war produced as a result of Western military policies and ideals, such as the landmark British documentary serial *The World at War* (1973), which does not feature a single episode devoted to conscientious objectors during World War II; or the absence of conscientious objectors in such serials as *The American Civil War* (2006). In both examples, the ideals of a specific Western policy of war-making were, and are, further militarized through television, and those who do not share such policies – conscientious objectors, for instance – are merely censored.

With the escalation of the contemporary technical beyond in the age of the aesthetics of disappearance, Virilio asserts, the two paradigms of the strategic event and of the age of imbalance are gaining theoretical and practical support, and their potential for the further militarization of television becomes more apparent. By contrast, Virilio proposes that we should avoid reducing television to a frightening escalation or to the display of famous onslaughts on tall buildings (essentially, military assaults that mark the beginning of the most recent age of imbalance). He argues that the new era of terrorism, with all its technical prostheses, is irreducible to the old era of terrorism, meaning that television is not just a matter of making programs about wars, or even of complying with those who make wars and programs about wars, but consists of being aware of the "recent revolution in weapons systems" and of the fact that they are "a mutation that is qualitative as well as quantitative" (2000c: 21). And so, as in the case of the Gulf War, Virilio's notion of television is founded on "the strategic emergence of 'communications weapons.'" Thus wars and killings today, in the landscapes of events, are not about "the traditional supremacy of 'weapons of destruction' or 'weapons of obstruction'." Rather, following "the three military fronts of land, sea, and air, we are seeing the gradual buildup of a fourth front: that of the power of information" (2000c: 21). For Virilio, television is based on the recognition that "international terrorism" is "inseparable from this *media front* and that terrorist attacks make sense and have political value only because of the televised publicity they invariably have at their disposal." The militarization of television occurs through the "telegenic quality of such atrocities constantly reinforcing their evocative power" (ibid.). It is of course prevented by the former Soviet Union and Italy, which have put comprehensive prohibitions on media coverage of terrorist carnage. To be aware of television is thus to be aware of the fact that the mass war of the armies of the twentieth century is being displaced by mass murderers who use the effect of the mass media to apply the utmost force on global public opinion.

This seems simple enough, but the repercussions of Virilio's perspective are multifaceted and extensive in the way they point toward a new conception of media events. This new conception is introduced in *A Landscape of Events*, but it is more systematically developed in his *City of Panic*.

CITY OF PANIC: THE INSTRUMENTAL IMAGE LOOP OF TELEVISION

Virilio's *City of Panic*, much like his *Ground Zero* (2002b) – which centers on posthuman "progress" as a kind of destructive force and on postmodern morals in the post-September 11, 2001 period of suicidal tendencies, dystopianism, and threats of all kinds – takes up again and expands several of the ideas in this earlier text, but it goes beyond *Ground Zero* in theorizing the contemporary fate of the age of the balance of terror, the landscape, cities, and media events.

City of Panic's title chapter (2005b: 85–112) starts with a series of illustrations like those cited in the last section, which identify an instant where what Virilio refers to as "fear" occurs: "'When fear takes hold of me, I make up an image,' wrote Goethe. No need to make up such mental imagery these days. The instrumental image is instantly provided for us by television" (p. 85). This quotation develops Virilio's assumptions about the trend toward the militarization of television in *A Landscape of Events*. To work from the viewpoint of the telegenic qualities of atrocities in the example taken from *A Landscape of Events*, the terroristic image is constantly reinforced and, more importantly here, fear emerges from the evocative power of that image. If we prevent the militarization of television by placing a comprehensive prohibition on media reporting of the most horrible terrorist killings, together with accidents, we increasingly become unaware of contemporary newsworthy events; but if we continually strengthen their inflammatory power we must lose out to the instrumental image that is instantaneously supplied to us by television. We are therefore prevented from stopping mass killers by using the influence of the mass media to wield maximum force on global public opinion.

Since there is no way for us to stop mass murderers by using the effect of the mass media and their power to exercise utmost coercion on public opinion worldwide, we are caught up in what Virilio calls "CITIES OF PANIC that signal, more clearly than all the theories about urban chaos, the fact that *the greatest catastrophe of the twentieth century has been the city*, the contemporary metropolis of the disasters of Progress" (p. 90). Connecting New York following the attack on the World Trade Center and its collapse on September 11, 2001 and Baghdad following the downfall of Saddam Hussein is a city of panic that, within the logics of contemporary warring city systems, cannot be reunited with the others because of the fear that divides them. The militarization of television thus continues to build walls in Hong Kong, Beijing, and beyond, while urban and rural people near the city find themselves bogged down in the logics of blockades and isolation, of airborne and warlike threats. Revisiting the categories of *The Aesthetics of Disappearance* for a moment, the militarization of television indicates once more the escalation of the modern technical beyond of "flying into the unknown" that is now at work among us in our major urban agglomerations. Actually, in *City of Panic*, the escalation of the technical beyond goes "on and on indefinitely." A war zone in all but name, militarized television not only contributes to the fear that presently grips the city of panic but also gestures, more obviously than all the hypotheses about metropolitan disorder, toward the fact that the supreme disaster of the twentieth and twenty-first centuries has been the city. According to Virilio, then, a city of panic is signaled by the present-day metropolis as the place of the failures of "progress." "This," he writes, emphasizing the fear factor and the constant fortification of terroristic images and their suggestive power, "is the real 'accident museum,' this megalopolis that takes itself for the navel, the *omphalos* of a finalized humanity" (p. 90). The telegenic qualities of atrocities, taking shape inside a "METACITY that no longer really takes *place*," are then continuously being bolstered by the evocative powers of militarized television, as fear and the logics of war take command in a city of panic that "now refuses to be located here or there the way the geopolitical capital of nations once used perfectly well to be."

Cities of panic are not only about war and urban fear, though. More particularly, Virilio depicts the city of panic as being related to the repetitious state of technical prostheses wherein "*the image loop has become the signature of contemporary disasters*" (p. 85). The city of panic is replete with instants that relentlessly emphasize the seductive power of terroristic images, a looping of the flow of techno-prosthetic images, where "the incessant round of satellites doing the ring road of the City-World is now doubled with the *looping* of terrorizing images in a state of siege of the viewer's mind." Virilio's city of panic thus indicates a place of "raging mass psychosis" where militarized television besieges and affects us all in the era of globalization, where the unremitting reinforcing of the evocative authority of terroristic images turns into fear. Furthermore, he asserts, these cities of panic are far more widespread than we might initially imagine. In the language of *A Landscape of Events*, a city of panic occurs when mass communications tools impose their militarized logics, values, and, crucially, their "*signature* on us," "in a bid to identify terror" and to prevent us from retaining our own emotions, our own, autonomous ways of knowing fear. All that is left is the sense that, ever since September 11, 2001, militarized television has taken all our emotions and fears prisoner.

Cities of panic are the departure point for Virilio's examination of the media events and philosophy of technical prostheses in *City of Panic*. He argues that the aim of media theory must be to try to "sniff out the building dangers" critically, given that viewers are now regularly subject "to the collective hallucination of a *single image*, the optical theatre of a revolving terrorist panorama" (p. 86). To investigate the implications that the city of panic generates for media theory, he produces a more complex and powerful theory of media technologies than that proposed through the idea of technical prostheses, which was employed in *The Aesthetics of Disappearance* and *A Landscape of Events*; and this new theory is what I call the instrumental image loop of television.

THE INSTRUMENTAL IMAGE LOOP OF TELEVISION, THEATRICAL MILITARISM, AND VISUAL DISCOURSES OF DISTRACTION

Virilio re-conceptualizes technical prostheses as the instrumental image loop of television, possibly to evade two potential misunderstandings that may have arisen from his past writings. First, the concept of technical prostheses implies that viewers are merely subject to "the reproduction of the stereotyped pictures Walter Benjamin [1968: 217–51] talked to us about" (2005b: 86); and, second, the idea of "technical prosthesis" is vague in that it can signify both separate forms of terrorism, such as the old or the new era of terrorism, and how these eras of terrorism are brought together to form discourses associated with the mechanical or digital reproduction and typecasting of images that make up many media events – for example that of September 11, 2001. Demonstrating how Virilio's deployment of a theory of the instrumental image loop of television surmounts these difficulties should serve to explain what I mean by the notion of "the instrumental image loop of television."

Initially, Virilio shifts from the concept of technical prostheses to that of the instrumental image loop of television in order to contest the preconception – rooted in the viewer by centuries of "the old iconoclasm of REPRESENTATION" and of representation "*in real space*" – that there are "painted" images, that there are "sculpted images," that painters, filmmakers, and so on utilize the old iconoclasm for their own symbolic ends (ibid.).

Representation, though, is merely one way of theorizing iconoclasm. Virilio argues that the instrumental image loop of television is a more direct point of departure, since what he calls the "iconoclasm of PRESENTATION *in real time* now outdoes by a long shot the old iconoclasm of REPRESENTATION *in real space* of painted or sculpted images" (ibid.). Who or what the "presentation" is always has to be demarcated or demonstrated, whether by the obliteration of the Buddhas of Bamian in Afghanistan, or by the pillaging of the National Museum of Iraq in Baghdad, and this is increasingly achieved through the instrumental image loop of television.

The instrumental image loop of television is not just an iconoclasm (while it can be that, too). It is any instance of the "panic symptom of a veritable *looping of the imaginary*" (ibid.). Thus it might be for instance the looped image of September 11, 2001, or "Operation Shock and Awe," which launched the Allied war on Iraq in 2003 and its live global TV coverage, but it might also be the looped image of a suicide bomber, of an Israeli military assault on Gaza, or of an atomic bomb's mushroom cloud – or any looped image presented by the global TV networks. Virilio argues that what we are witnessing is a mutation involving the instrumental image loop of television: a mutation which means that, today, a "SIEGE PSYCHOSIS" is afflicting our state of mind. The panic symptomatic of the instrumental image loop of television "is the first sign typical of a FORECLOSURE that is temporal": according to Virilio, the global TV networks that present the instrumental image loop of television are conducting a kind of "experiment" on their viewers. The instrumental image loop of television is thus presented as a sort of "life-size TEST, of globalization," a loop that is associated with a cybernetic vision and a "political gothic" (pp. 86–7). Such instants of panic are the basic ingredients of "the management of public fear, which kicked off some forty years ago" with "the balance of terror" and which has been "back on active duty" since September 11, 2001 (p. 87). In other words, if we take the instrumental image loop of "Operation Shock and Awe," the global TV networks were the ones that produced "a real multimedia 'magic show,'" the viewers were the people to whom it was emitted, the life-size test of globalization was "Operation Shock and Awe," and the cybernetic vision and political gothic consisted in the fact that the life-size test of globalization was the captivation of "the hordes with a welter of pyrotechnical tricks." Each instant of panic is presented in real time through the instrumental image loop of television, which forms a particular configuration involving the management of public fear. None of these instants of panic pre-exists the instrumental image loop of television or is its source; instead, each comes into being in an instant, just as the instrumental image loop of television occurs. From Virilio's standpoint, viewers are used and abused by the global TV networks' huge arsenal of "weapons of mass communication" and life-size tests of globalization take form as effects of the relation between instrumental image loops of television, cybernetic vision, and the political gothic.

What becomes the center of Virilio's argument is how the instrumental image loop of television is connected to the collective hallucination of a single image. He argues that it is essential to consider the collective hallucination of a single image in conjunction with the instrumental image loop of television: he responds to this "bunch of tricks" by focusing on its mutation in relation to the instrumental image loop of television (p. 88). Here his response is to contemplate the United States and the pretense involved in its "wild escapade in the biblical desert," as, for him, it is becoming increasingly impossible to respond to any given instrumental image loop of television in any other way than the one intended. In discussing the instrumental image loop of the globally televised "assault on Baghdad," which "ended in the demolition of his [Saddam Hussein's] statue in Fardus Square," for example, he notes that it was "televised live and in a loop, before the eyes of the whole world while, more discreetly, off-camera, the sack of Sumerian marvels was in train." Each of these connections to the collective hallucination of a single image implies very similar things: "consent" to "the 'decapitation operation' perpetrated on the effigy of Saddam Hussein," lack of argument about the wisdom of cybernetic vision or the political gothic of putting capital cities under siege (the globally televised assault on Baghdad), international "agreement" on the life-size test of globalization (it is the "reconstruction" of Baghdad rather than the demolition of Saddam's statue), or even a change of the life-size test of globalization from the destruction of Saddam's statue to the other – possibly myriad, yet somehow identical – instrumental looping images of the global TV networks, which amount to little more than the mounting of a theatrical stage set. There is thus a connection with the collective hallucination of a single image, and similar ways of connecting cybernetic vision and the political gothic take the image in very similar directions.

In reflecting on this issue of how the collective hallucination of a single image is connected to the instrumental image loop of television, Virilio settles another question, concerning the vagueness of technical prostheses – the fact that the category "technical prosthesis" is too wide-ranging and indistinct because it refers to various types of technical prostheses and their relation to the old and new eras of terrorism, and also to more general visual discourses – such as the Americans knocking over the statue of Saddam Hussein in Baghdad's Fardus Square, where, "'after a lot of rallying by loudspeaker, there were about hundred'" Iraqis – "*just enough for the television pictures*'" (Sitz, cited at p. 89). Virilio distinguishes between what Emmanuel Todd (cited at p. 88) calls "theatrical militarism," which refers to deception in the military theater of operations, and what I call "visual discourses of distraction," which refers to the televisually and militarily directed organization of communications. The seemingly different yet actually very similar forms of theatrical militarism, which include the old and new eras of terrorism, are all similar ways of relating the instants of panic that are essential elements in the management of public fear. Similar forms of theatrical militarism thus present sets of relations between the instants of panic and fear that are similar to those marked in an instrumental image loop of television. For instance, the relationships between the global TV networks and their viewers is similar to those among the members of a theatrical company mounting a stage set; or the relations between cybernetic vision, the political gothic, and the life-size test of globalization are similar to what happened after the fall of Saddam Hussein's statue:

"The Hotel Palestine turned into a kind of theatre. From the balcony, you could see scenes being set up expressly for us, Caroline Sitz, of French television channel, France 3, explained, her conclusion being: 'You never did see pictures of the battle of Baghdad, in any case.'" (Sitz, cited at p. 89)

This means, Virilio argues, that instrumental image loops of television are the similar products of a theatrical militarism, which are transferable from one theater of military operations to another (p. 89). This is a more precise account of the argument in *A Landscape of Events* about the mutation of terrorism: each instant of theatrical militarism forms instrumental image loops of television seemingly differently yet actually very similarly, and it is thus impossible for instrumental image loops of television in one instant of theatrical militarism to be different, even if they occur in another theater of military operations.

Visual discourses of distraction are similar to theatrical militarism, and they are ways of organizing, for example, the turning of our attention away from the "War on Terrorism" and toward the war against Iraq. "Distraction," Virilio argues, "is exactly the word most appropriate" to describe not so much the logic of the collective hallucination of a single image or the instrumental image loop of television as that particular form of theatrical militarism "whereby the United States struts around bragging shamelessly while the world implodes in silence" (p. 105). Stated another way, a particular visual discourse of distraction such as the *"outrageous bluster"* of "the sending to Iraq of the National Guard of Florida" employed the instrumental image loop of television through a form of theatrical militarism that sought to achieve a particular end: to obtain "order" in Baghdad. Such visual discourses of distraction employ the instrumental image loop of television in ways similar to those of theatrical militarism, and their end is similar too: to divert attention away from the fact that, for instance, "'civil peace' is no more guaranteed now by the law than the state of peace between nations is guaranteed by international organizations" such as the United Nations. Similar visual discourses of distraction have similar criteria for judging the value of particular ways of invoking the collective hallucination of a single image and the instrumental image loop of television, and each visual discourse of distraction discourages certain forms of collective imagery. In the "outrageous bluster" of "the sending to Iraq of the National Guard of Florida," for instance, it was not considered "legitimate" by the US military to regard this collective imagery and its instrumental image loop of television in relation to the fact that this unit seemed "just as much at ease in the suburbs of the Iraqi capital as in the slums of America," as to do so would immediately take one outside the visual discourse of distraction that was the "outrageous bluster" and into questions about American civilian populations, about their recurrent looting and their habitual violence. A visual discourse of distraction is thus a means of giving legitimacy to particular types of collective hallucinations, single images, and of organizing instrumental image loops of television into "a DISTRACTION, a bout of showbiz that has diverted attention away from chaos that is obviously here to stay" (p. 108).

The instrumental image loop of television consequently carries with it much more visual information than just what it shows: by connecting the instant of panic, by fitting into theatrical militarism, and by being focused toward a purpose through visual discourses of distraction, it inaugurates a world of synchronized emotions.

According to Virilio, instrumental image loops of television are instants of illusion, plays "being performed before [our] disbelieving eyes": "at all costs, that is [. . .] the tele-objective of the contemporary mass media" (2007a: 20). Furthermore, because of the global TV networks' need for the collective hallucination produced by the single image, for the instrumental image loop of television, the question of how instrumental image loops of television maintain the collective "harmony" of what Virilio calls "the synchronization of emotions" (p. 21) is, for him, always associated with the severe censorship of media events. This is how he investigates media events in *The Original Accident* (2007a).

THE INSTRUMENTAL IMAGE LOOP OF TELEVISION, MEDIA EVENTS, AND THE SYNCHRONIZATION OF EMOTIONS

For Virilio, media events are not simply one visual discourse of distraction among others. Instead, media events emerge in and from every decision made by the global TV networks about how to produce the collective hallucination of a single image and the instrumental image loop of television. Such choices occur within always already existing visual discourses of distraction and are thus bound up with the logics of particular visual discourses of distraction, with the collective hallucination of a single image and its aims. Virilio argues that, since September 11, 2001, visual discourses of distraction have imposed their mode of collective hallucination and the single image onto our perceptions through the instrumental image loop of television, since "media coverage of acts of violence has everywhere expanded" (2007a: 20). This violence is the city of panic, since visual discourses of distraction and "the accumulation of felonies of a different nature has little by little given the impression that all forms of protection collapsed at the same time as the World Trade Center." Every time a specific collective hallucination is made into a single image, all other potential collective images – the images that are not promoted by the visual discourses of distraction within which the global TV networks are functioning – are ruthlessly repressed. While there will always be many potential collective images and many possible responses, only the hallucination of the single image actually and increasingly materializes. This twists every collective hallucination, every single image, into a sort of "dramatic portrayal" that "has created, in televiewers, a twin fear, a stereo-anxiety" whereby visual discourses of distraction escalate the dread felt about "public insecurity." Such dread "has been topped up with fear of the images of 'audiovisual' insecurity, bringing about a sudden highlighting of domestic terror, designed to intensify collective anguish." This alarm, public anxiety, horror, panic, and suffering are not without repercussions. On deciding to appeal to this "mute cry of the hordes of the absent," the global and increasingly militarized TV networks must choose a precise instrumental image loop of television, which repulses all other potential "civilian" collective images and which has its audiences "all present at the same moment in front of their screens contemplating disaster, stunned" (ibid.).

This dramatic portrayal, twin fear, or stereo-anxiety associated with the instrumental image loop of television and with the collective hallucination of a single image is the starting point for an understanding of media events in the city of panic. Indeed, it is a conception of media events that appears with the advent of the instrumental image loop of television:

> The sudden stereoscopic highlighting of the event, accident or attack, thus well and truly amounts to the birth of a new type of tragedy, one not only audiovisual, but binocular and stereophonic, in which the perspective of the real time of synchronized emotions produces the submission of consciences to this "terrorism in evidence" – that we see with our own eyes – that further enhances the authority of the media. (Virilio 2007a: 21)

Each collective hallucination of a single image is a media event, as it is founded on the decision of the global TV networks to invoke the collective hallucination of a single image of a calamity or of an urban offensive. In every collective hallucination of the single image, all of the other audiovisual possibilities for collective imagery are rejected or suppressed, and the possible appearance of other collective images not founded on the binocular, stereophonic, and real-time perspective of synchronized emotions is refused.

Questions of obedient consciences, terrorism, perception, and the power of media events, at their most important level, thus occur ubiquitously: there is no mass or individual decision, act, incident, or mediated text that is not in some way connected to the authority of the media event as it is bound up with the city of panic. In many instances, the investments in this media event might appear unimportant, but in others the consequences of a single instrumental image loop of television can change lives and cultures through the sudden appearance and disappearance of catastrophes and atrocities all across the world.

The task of the media theorist, according to Virilio (pp. 20–1), is to expose the uncertain instants where the city of panic occurs and something has been masked, and to discover ways to make visible what is presently invisible and imposed on everybody: our responsibility before endlessly repetitive images of a fear we are completely enthralled by consists in revealing the city of panic itself and in declaring that it is here "where the future is played out between the menace of a single person and the war of each against all" in the age of the instrumental image loop of television. This is not simply a question of a "stasis that democracy must protect itself from every bit as much as the lone tyrant," of a city of panic that, in the era of globalization, resorts to visual discourses of distraction founded on the real time of telecommunications with logics applicable to today's public screens – visual discourses of distraction through "which the 'people's acts' are played out" (p. 19). Instead, it is a case of asserting or declaring the reality of the city of panic as a litany of images, as a "liturgy where repeat catastrophes and cataclysms have the role of some *deus ex machina*, if not of the oracle announcing the horrors to come and denouncing, thereby, the abomination of the destiny of the peoples" and searching for new forms and languages through which to escape the dictatorship of the instrumental image loop of television. This, he argues, is the role of the critic of the art of technology: what is in the balance with television, with "hundreds of millions of people" seeing "the same event at the same moment in time," with media events, is the emergence of a city of panic "with the same kind of dramatic performance as at the theater in days not long gone" (pp. 19–20).

CONCLUSION

Virilio is primarily a theorist of media events, and this influences all of his interpretations of cities, panic, and television. *A Landscape of Events* examines the possibility of theorizing television following the escalation of the modern technical beyond of "flying into the unknown." His ideas concerning the mutation of terrorism argue that it is dangerous to base one's choices about the landscape of events on concepts focused on the conventional preeminence of "weapons of destruction" and "weapons of obstruction." Rather, he offers a perspective on the landscape of events rooted in the recognition of the part played by technical prostheses and by the realities of the post-Cold War international order. The militarization of television transpires when other, "civilian" ways of televised perception are blacked out by our technical prostheses becoming dominated by the glorification of the ideals of the professional military classes and terrorism.

City of Panic and *The Original Accident* are two of Virilio's principal books. Here he develops a more multifaceted idea of technical prostheses, founded on what I have called the instrumental image loop of television. The focal point of these books' investigations gradually becomes the question of how the instrumental image loop of television is connected to the collective hallucination of a single image and what the consequences of increasingly similar collective images might be. Instrumental image loops of television, according to Virilio, are classified into theatrical militarism (such as the fall of Saddam Hussein's statue) and visual discourses of distraction (such as the "outrageous bluster" of "the sending to Iraq of the National Guard of Florida"), which produce sets of principles by which the collective hallucination of a single image and of instrumental image loops of television is organized into a militarized and televised form of distraction. The media exposure of acts of aggression and its growth through visual discourses of distraction is the space wherein decisions about media events are made, as the global TV networks decide between the ever more similar possibilities for the instrumental image loops of television they encourage and the possible alternative images they deter us from. Virilio argues that, each time the instrumental image loops of television are connected to the collective hallucination of a single image, that is the foundation for an appreciation of media events in the city of panic. He describes the synchronized emotions of the city of panic as an instant at which the surrender of consciences to terrorism is placed in a position where it is impossible to flee the despotism of the instrumental image loop of television; and he argues that it is in the cities of panic that the critique of the art of technology that is television must commence.

5

THE WORK OF THE CRITIC OF THE ART OF TECHNOLOGY

The Museum of Accidents

INTRODUCTION

This final chapter brings back together our diverse discussions of Virilio's *Aesthetics of Disappearance* and his conception of the media. It explores the connotations of the aesthetics of disappearance and introduces ideas about the kind of critical responses that Virilio encourages us to have to contemporary art and technology.

Each of the previous four chapters concluded by arguing that Virilio's media theory produces ways to undermine and disturb those systematic theories that seek to offer "transparent" or "positive" accounts, be they theories of aesthetics, cinema, new media, or the city. The main goal of Virilio's media theory is to allow distinctive images, voices, and novel ways of reflecting, writing, and behaving in the world to appear through these disturbances. By presenting the world as we see it and its passing, the aesthetics of picnolepsy can change recognized ways of writing about technical prostheses or about subliminally picturing the image world, and it can join in techno-social, futuristic, and aesthetic debates over disappearance. By theorizing about the cinema in relation to war, the critic of the art of technology can herald new potentialities for a logistics-based media theory and action and can permit those aesthetic images and voices susceptible of disappearance to be seen and heard. Study of new media can determine those points at which the modern technical beyond of "flying into the unknown," of the age of the aesthetics of disappearance, is escalated; and ways are opened to more critical methods of considering vision technologies, polar inertia, and the accident. Examination of the city of panic, television, and media events can change recognized methods of theorizing the contemporary urban landscape, re-imagine the domain of terrorism, and contribute to discussions about theatrical militarism, visual discourses of distraction, and the synchronization of emotions. In all of these instances, the occurrence of an aesthetic instant of disappearance, of a logistics of perception, or of an accident has the standing of a media event. Extremely difficult to forecast in the city of panic, a media event such as September 11, 2001 occurs that is irreducible to conventional critical or visual analysis, and this requires an understanding of, for example, the instrumental image loop of television.

It is clear that Virilio's conclusions across various discussions have deep significance for how we theorize contemporary mediated life. However, certain readers are left with the irksome misgiving that something is absent. Virilio reveals the instants and methods where media discourses are exposed to disturbance, and objections are raised as to the authority and the escalation of the modern technical beyond. Nonetheless, his work presents very little regarding an agenda for media theory or practice in response to such instants. Now that we have uncovered the logistics of perception, for instance, what shall we do with it?

Virilio's ostensible refusal to supply some direction for coping with media events, or even to specify a method into which they can be introduced, has irritated some of his critics. For example, Nigel Thrift (2011: 145–57) complains about the obstacle of a clear-cut application of Virilio's media theory to social science. "Virilio's relentless negativism about the future in the present," he writes, "does not seem to me to constitute an answer." Indeed, for Thrift, Virilio's "brand of doom-saying" is "profoundly out of kilter with prevalent tendencies on the left that are moving toward putting far more emphasis on constructing a politics of hope than before" (p. 147). Thrift's dilemma is that Virilio's concentration on "negativism" seems to preclude the option of "an answer," in addition to not allowing the critic a capacity to engender "a politics of hope" concerned with how "the left" should occupy the future. Thrift concludes that "writers like Virilio" must be brought "back to everyday life in all its everydayness" (p. 154), and he advocates an acknowledgment of the significance of maintaining the critical processes of a social scientific idea of everyday life. Thrift's analysis, and the defense of everyday life to which it points, are not only aimed at Virilio's supposed aloofness and retreat from everyday life through the discipline of social science: they might also apply to most of Virilio's arguments about the aesthetics of disappearance. All of the debates in the earlier chapters have concluded with an instant of disturbance. Yet a question arises: What comes after that? What does Virilio advise us about how we should understand an aesthetic image, interpret a work of cinema, study new media, or even resist the city of panic? What are we meant to accomplish with the aesthetics of disappearance, the logistics of perception, the accident, and media events?

These are vital and real questions. Critically, though, they are ones that Virilio only partially sets out to answer. He does adopt a specific aesthetic methodology, that of building "The Museum of Accidents" (Virilio 2003b: 58–65; Virilio and Lotringer 2005: 91–112; Virilio 2007a: 23–30), even if he does not take up a particular technological credo any more than he offers absolute or unquestionable theories of aesthetics. There is, then, no "Virilian" method: he does not supply beforehand Thrift's "answer" to the possible questions created by aesthetic theory and media events. Actually, from the previous discussions in this book it should be obvious that there could not possibly be such a method: to establish a Virilian method would be to negate Virilio's most important observations about the logistics of perception, accidents, and media events. Such a method would, to employ the etymology of the word accident, presuppose *"what has happened"* (see Virilio and Lotringer 2005: 101). Put differently, it would explicate the importance of an accident or media event before it happened, and thus it would eradicate its transformative possibility by installing it into what is already known, into what has happened before. To understand Virilio, we must allow for this partial refusal to presuppose accidents, media events, and the logistics of perception. If we are to nurture his media theory, what is necessary is an awareness of real time, of the accident, and attention to the potentialities that the instant of the accident or the unexpected media events' disturbance of long-established civilizations might disclose. This is simultaneously annoying – because Virilio offers us only one partial answer – and stimulating – because it compels us to dwell on the Museum of Accidents.

The question that this chapter will take up, therefore, is the following: What is the work of the critic of the art of technology, or of the media theorist, as it is conceptualized

in Virilio's writings? What openings do his writings produce
for others' aesthetic, technological, or critical examinations
and deliberations? The chapter summarizes Virilio's aesthetic perspective on media theory, his arguments about
the difference between critical and uncritical approaches to
contemporary art and technology, and his endorsement of
the former as an instrument for critical thought about the
media. The chapter then considers Virilio's investigations
concerning the significance of approaching critically art,
technology, and culture; and it considers his critique of the
accident. Finally, it discusses his aesthetic critique through
an examination of the Museum of Accidents and his recent
writings in *Art as Far as the Eye Can See* (2007b), to offer an
illustration of his method of rethinking the art museum and
the accident through an interpretation of his "The Night of
the Museums" (in 2007b: 69–114).

AN AESTHETIC PERSPECTIVE ON MEDIA THEORY: CRITICAL AND UNCRITICAL APPROACHES TO CONTEMPORARY ART AND TECHNOLOGY

As I have made it clear, the impact of aesthetics on Virilio
is substantial. Over and above any other concept, he returns
constantly to aesthetics to establish the implements for
theorizing about contemporary media, art, and technology.
We have already reflected on the significance, for Virilio,
of aesthetic distinctions between concepts of appearance
and ideas of disappearance, cinema and war, and his examinations of the logistics of perception, new media, vision,
inertia, the accident, cities, panic, television, and media
events. Still, there is one contention of his concerning
aesthetics that is even more important for his creation of
an aesthetic perspective on media theory: the difference

between uncritical and critical approaches to present-day art and technology.

As we saw in the Introduction, the idea of a critical viewpoint on contemporary art and technology is advanced by Virilio in his and Sylvère Lotringer's *Pure War* to clarify the way he reacts to current aesthetic and technological experiences, but its consequences are much broader than simply to produce theories about media, art, and technology. As stated in *Pure War*, critical approaches to contemporary art and technology involve the ability to think of art and technology as "asymptotic to everything" (Virilio and Lotringer 2008: 192). This last formulation purely means that a critical standpoint on prevailing art and technology appreciates them as a trajectory, which continually moves toward the curve of "everything" we call "reality," but which in fact never meets it because it is frequently prone to collapse before it arrives there. Being asymptotic to everything, and in particular to recent cultural logics, technological principles, and aesthetic traditions, means that perceptions of contemporary art and technology, according to Virilio, must not be understood through an uncritical outlook, especially regarding new kinds of art and technology. Certainly, for him, to think about art and technology is not only to consider postmodern art and technology as such but, crucially, to contemplate them as asymptotic to everything – from a strongly critical stance. The foundation of Virilio's attitude to the latest art and technology, from this point of view, is the result of an association between specific perceptions or experiences of art and technology and the fact that they are asymptotic to everything, a conception that permits media theorists like Virilio to recognize them and to reveal what art and technology in reality are. So, to acknowledge a specific piece of art as a painting, we must be capable of relating the sensation of that art object to the concept of a "painting."

This idea is asymptotic to everything since it can be related to all of the diverse paintings that we encounter, notwithstanding the artistic and technological differences between them. Whether it is a portrait or a landscape, a canvas or a mural painting, a work framed in wood or in metal, we must nevertheless be capable of incorporating it into the concept of a "painting" if we are to recognize it. Thus an approach to contemporary art and technology is what determines which aesthetic and technological discourses will be appropriate to describe and appreciate art, technology, and their present conditions.

The distinction between an uncritical and a critical approach to contemporary art and technology transpires from the diverse means by which this connection between ideas of media and experiences of art and technology occurs. An uncritical perspective on postmodern art and technology, which is actually of the kind we embrace more or less continually, takes place when we instate a new aesthetic or technological experience into our present conceptual arrangements. This denotes that uncritical approaches to contemporary art and technology are apt to be procedures of identification. Hence our recognition or identification of something transpires from our aptitude to link a specific aesthetic or technological experience of it to ideas that we had previously. For instance we can recognize and identify a specific boxed technological system for converting visual images endowed with sound into electrical signals, for transmitting them by radio or other means, and for displaying them electronically on a screen, because we already have an idea of what a television set is. We are able to do this almost unthinkingly: the television set in front of us appears to be spontaneously just what it is.

Against uncritical viewpoints on recent art and technology, critical approaches express or involve an analysis of the merits and faults of a new work of art or of an unusual or unfamiliar technology, an examination that typically incorporates a detailed and scholarly investigation and commentary, and we strive to cope with what they are or signify. The particular expression is experienced and we are compelled to look for a method of relating ourselves to it or of conceptually scrutinizing its strengths and weaknesses. This may happen concerning developments in contemporary art or technology that confuse our imaginative outlook. Certainly, Virilio argues that this has ensued in all aesthetic and technological experiences over the last century, particularly when we are challenged by those events that are materializing as our cultural nightmare – and with which we are increasingly familiar thanks to Virilio's scorching visions of art and technology as competing with each other for the obliteration of the human form. Our current conceptual norms appear not to be relevant to the particular situation; so, sooner than using them, we consider contemporary art and technology critically and try to find the links that will make things such as avant-garde art seem sensible and direct our reactions to them. Regarding Virilio, I argue that his critical approach to postmodern art and technology cannot be located in one artistic subject, technological sphere, or aesthetic method alone, but makes clear and forges interdisciplinary links among all of them. It is therefore always essential to reflect on advanced art and technology without preconditions, yet critically. For Virilio, the significance of a critical approach to present-day art and technology is increasingly tied to aesthetic discourses of the human form, to a critical angle on the "progressive" art of disappearance and to the technologies of abstraction and war. Virilio (2003a: back cover) argues that a critical approach to existing art and technology must connect, for example, the diverse discourses of the "German Expressionists' hate-filled portraits of the damned" through "the 'medical' experiments of the Nazi eugenicists" or, instead, through "the mangled messages of sensationalist advertising and the organization of global terrorism." Consequently, in the twenty-first century, when technology at last "leaves art behind as genetic engineers prepare to turn themselves into the worst of expressionists," a critical outlook on cutting-edge art and technology is needed more than ever. Any appreciation of postmodern art manifestos, of the Human Genome Project, and of the contemporary "human being, the raw material for new and monstrous forms of life," must be generated by a critical approach to contemporary art and technology and to media theory. Without such a point of view we are trapped within the connected logics and arrangements of a twentieth-century art or media theory while the trajectories of technology are taking us into the next phase of the aesthetics of disappearance or of the modern technical beyond of "flying into the unknown."

One way to specify the connotations of the differences between uncritical and critical approaches to contemporary art and technology is to turn to "A Pitiless Art" that Virilio explains in *Art and Fear* (2003a: 27–65). Confronted with the pitilessness of the twentieth century, Virilio thoughtfully contemplates the "pitiless nature of 'contemporary art'" and technology. Avoiding the (by now) uncritical distinction between profane and sacred art, Virilio follows his own trajectory. In fact, he lays down new examples concerning "the profanation of forms and bodies over the course of the twentieth century," because "these days when people [. . .] debate the relevance or awfulness of contemporary art, they generally forget to ask one vital question: *Contemporary art, sure, but contemporary with what?*" Effectively, in adopting a critical view on modern-day art and technology, Virilio asks whether the "Nazi terror" of World War II is still at work in "the forms and figures" of postmodern art and technology.

In taking up this approach to contemporary art and technology, he responds critically to the "universality of the extermination of bodies, as well as of the environment, from AUSCHWITZ to CHERNOBYL." Here he endeavors to look for a trajectory wherein our current dehumanization from without, our shattered ethical and aesthetic bearings, and "our very perception of our surroundings" can be articulated. Clearly, this is not an easy choice. All of his critical faculties concerning present-day art and technology are exercised, in addition to his critique of industrial modernity and – conceivably – its artistic and technological legacies; and there are no assurances that any "answer" acceptable to Thrift or any other critics of art and technology will be unearthed. Aesthetically, though, he argues that any critical approach to contemporary art is obligated to confront the trajectories of technology and warfare. It must analyze up-to-the-minute art and technology from the perspective of the "wound" and not of the "knife," of the "bayonet," of "Oskar Kokoschka, 'the scalpel-wielding artist,'" of the "German Expressionism of Der Sturm," and of the "Viennese Actionism" of the 1960s. This is because to stay within the uncritical view of the latest art and technology exhibited in the postmodern art world would be to censor, for example, the fact that Richard Hülsenbeck, "one of the founding fathers of Dada," was actually an artist who favored World War I. Such a credulous perspective would obviously condemn Virilio to an uncritical or "silent" position on Dada's previously unremarked upon historic role in the endorsement of war.

A critical approach to contemporary art and technology is then central to Virilio's media theory. He argues that such an approach is the paradigm for an aesthetic perspective on media theory. The work of media theory is to respond critically to events that occur in order to try to discern new logics and ways of behaving in the present day. Art and aesthetics,

as was argued in the first four chapters, are important loca-
tions from which critique can appear. Artistic, aesthetic, or
technological appearance and disappearance have the possibility to disrupt recognized media theoretical discourses and,
because of their event-based nature, they contest previously
acknowledged methods of considering and understanding
the world of media. Considered critically, art and aesthetics can astonish us and open up new potentialities for media
theory. However, if we adopt uncritical approaches, which
are merely applied in order to evaluate art and technology
indiscriminatingly, what is demanding, astounding, and possibly transformative in contemporary art and technology
disappears. The aesthetic critic of the art of technology, as
indicated by Virilio, should be capable of approaching contemporary art and technology critically and be receptive to
their standing as what I call a "trajective event."

ART, TECHNOLOGY, AND CULTURE: VIRILIO'S
CRITIQUE OF THE ACCIDENT

The main reason why Virilio turns to a critical approach to
art evolves from his study of the arrangements of contemporary technology and culture and from his critique of the
modern technical beyond. For Virilio, the media theorist
or critic of the art of technology cannot be a person who
positions him- or herself beyond the difficulties of art, technology, and culture. No one is equipped to consider them
in "God's eye," neutral terminology, from the standpoint of
some supremely accurate postmodern perspective on artistic,
technological, and cultural discourses that is able to systematize all other media texts, aesthetic contexts, and trajective
technological and cultural events into a grand philosophical schema. Every mass or "massified" individual subsists as
an element of a "technoculture" (Shaw 2008) whose leading

artistic, technological, and cultural discourses form the way
we observe our civilization. That is why art, technology, and
culture are not expressions or objects that are appended to
a pre-recognized massified individual. Instead, art, technology, and culture are what influences us and what makes us
into massified individuals. Moreover, this is just as accurate
of postmodern art, technology, and culture now as it was of
art, technology, and culture long ago. In a recent chapter
entitled "Caution," Virilio describes twenty-first-century art
in the era of technoculture as an effort to "promote artistic torture, aesthetic self-mutilation and suicide" (2007a: 8).
Massified individuals develop from how they reciprocally
appreciate those crucial instants in art, such as the encouragement of aesthetic agony. Massified individuals do not
deliberately take on this communal aesthetic awareness.
Rather, such aesthetic knowledge shapes the spirit of what we
imagine ourselves to be and supplies the essential structures
of how, in his example, they intersect with self-destruction.
This is how he characterizes twenty-first century art and
technoculture. Consequently contemporary art, technology,
and culture are not a "pitiful" (in the sense of arousing or
deserving compassion) aesthetic discovery or explanation of
well-balanced technocultural relations, which are supple-
mentary to massified individual experience and explain for
instance how people, even uncritically, distinguish between
profane and sacred art. Alternatively, current art, technology, and culture are precisely those means of connecting that
happen regardless of whether or not they are comprehended
or formally acknowledged as the endorsement of what the
American artist Joy Garnett calls the "apocalyptic sublime"
(Armitage and Garnett 2011: 59–78)) of creative torment,
and made into logics of artistic disfigurement and self-
annihilation as art forms.

This insight into what art, technology, and culture are persists all through Virilio's work. It is most obviously explained in his reflections on the traditional type of technological systematization, which was considered in Chapter 1. There, in Virilio's account of Eve, the first woman, it is comparatively easy to understand how the performance of Eve's technocultural or "logistical role" is produced by her anticipation of the later accomplishments of "technical media," wherein Eve's and others' attitudes toward technology, sexual characteristics, and seductive relations are linked to those of her spouse, Adam. Woman's emergence is positioned in relation to Satan, who materializes in the Bible as her seducer, and the important trajective events of her existence are those pertaining to the seduction of man. In this regard, Eve's character grows from this collective culture constructed in her launching of the reproductive and technological cycle of the human race.

However, in accident-prone contemporary civilizations, this idea of a logistical role in technoculture is a great deal more challenging. In "Caution," Virilio argues that we are becoming accelerated as art, technology, and culture succumb to the "gradual spread of catastrophic events" – a spread that "not only affects the reality of the moment but causes anxiety and anguish for generations to come" (2007a: 3). This conception of accidents as the slow advance of technological catastrophes and machinic cataclysms into the sphere of human individuality and everyday life ought to be recognizable from our considerations of *The Aesthetics of Disappearance, War and Cinema, The Vision Machine*, and *City of Panic* in previous chapters. In all of these texts Virilio explores and interrogates the accident's means of connecting art and technology to culture. He works out the repercussions of contemporary changes in our experience, where massified individual survival is downgraded to merely another feature of a postmodern system whose solitary objective is to maximize the "propaganda of twentieth-century progress" (Virilio and Armitage 2009: 107). The purpose of his writing and the rationale for its concentration on *"what has happened"* and on the acceleration of temporality is to confront the relegation of customs and morality, art, politics, and nationhood to the sole measure of speed.

AESTHETIC CRITIQUE: THE MUSEUM OF ACCIDENTS

In an important book entitled *The Original Accident*, Virilio investigates how "the threat of the unexpected" (2007a: 3) can be employed by the critic of the art of technology to oppose the demotion of art and culture to computations of instantaneous technologies in contemporary civilization.

Virilio argues that accidents and speed can be recognized and delineated as visibly postmodern characteristics, where speed always comes before the accident. Accordingly, for Virilio, speed is usually implicated in the accident. This argument resembles his scrutiny of the association between the transfer accident and speed in *Polar Inertia*, which we discussed in Chapter 3. He combines the two as distinctive present-day traits and portrays them as pitting themselves against existing civilization. His process of uniting these two attributes in *The Original Accident* concentrates on how they connect with the temporality of the trajective event. He examines this connection with the boundedness of time and with the trajective event through a refusal of "powerlessness in the face of the surging up of unexpected and catastrophic events," by "throwing open the doors of the first Museum of Accidents," and by undertaking "the *imperative of responsibility* for the generations to come" (pp. 4–7).

In two key chapters of *The Original Accident* – "Caution" and "The Accident Museum" – Virilio elucidates the place that each of the concepts in these two titles inhabit in his media theory and practice. His repudiation of helplessness despite unforeseen and disastrous trajective events develops from an attempt to overturn the customary tendency that exposes us to the accident (p. 4). Consequently, to take up his example from "Caution," he is seeking "to establish a new kind of museology or museography: one that would now entail exposing the accident [. . .] from the most banal to the most tragic, from natural catastrophes to industrial and scientific disasters." His notion of the work of critics of the art of technology is that they must open the first Museum of Accidents with an eye to rejecting their and our subjection to sudden and shattering trajective events. In opening the Museum of Accidents, he thinks that it is time to institute a "museum to what crops up impromptu, to that 'indirect production' of science and the technosciences constituted by disasters, by industrial or other catastrophes." He declares that there is a pressing need to reverse a tendency that consists in exposing us to the most disastrous accidents emanating from technoscience. Thus he maintains that current experience has revealed to him that we must "kick-start" an "approach which would consist in exposing the accident – exhibiting it – as the major enigma of modern progress." As a result, he presents the idea of what he calls "the imperative of responsibility for the generations to come." Now, instead of merely accepting accidents as a "normal" part of modern everyday life, the critique of the art of technology consists in renouncing our defenselessness, notwithstanding the appearance of bewildering and calamitous trajective events, to "expose accidents along with the frequency of their industrial and post-industrial repetition." "This," he asserts, was "the whole point" of his "exhibition at the *Fondation Cartier pour l'art contemporain* [2003b] as well as its avowed aim." In assuming the imperative of responsibility for the generations to come, he argues for a rehearsal of a future Museum of Accidents. This last entails, as he contends in "Caution," that the exhibition and, by implication, his own future critical work, "aims first and foremost to take a stand against the collapse of ethical and aesthetic landmarks, that loss of meaning we so often witness now as victims much more than as actors."

Virilio develops the idea of opening the Museum of Accidents and takes on the imperative of responsibility for the generations to come through his aesthetic critique of the technological accident and speed. A critic of the accident, he argues, is duty-bound to open the Museum of Accidents in order to make it "act as a counterpoint to the outrages of all stripes that we are swamped with on a daily basis by the major media outlets" (2007a: 8). It would be similar to a "museum of horrors." Neither the media nor anyone else seems to understand that today's accidents precede and accompany the escalation of even larger tragedies. Therefore what Virilio extracts from his explanation concerning the opening of the Museum of Accidents is that the critic of the art of technology brings the trajective event that is the accident into an explanatory discourse. The accident is exposed through museological study and, like the public horrified by contemporary disasters, its ambiguous exhibition and the previously unknown tribulations it creates are examined. Regarding the contemporary media theorist of the accident or the critic of the art of technology, this indicates that the trajective event that is being evaluated is endowed with some sort of clarification rather than with none. Yet, in incorporating the precise discourse of the trajective event, Virilio also insists on maintaining a critical distance from resentments of every sort. Virilio's example of this method is his critical examination of postmodern civilization, where he discovers the question of the unforeseen and, having exposed it, argues

THE MUSEUM OF ACCIDENTS

that he has identified and condemned the inattentiveness to major risks from which the accident exhibition and its manifesto are produced: the paying of homage to aesthetic judgment. Moreover, as in the museum of horrors, Virilio argues that, by disclosing present-day "intelligence" as fatally flawed, he allows us to recover *"preventive intelligence."* A critical study of the accident is appropriate, therefore, because, as he argues, in discovering the public horror of the threats of contemporary civilization, it offers one response to culture's increasingly militarized troubles and, from this, it advances a different description of the future as a dystopian civilization equipped and trained for war. In other words, it hypothesizes the coming total destruction of the modern technical beyond of "flying into the unknown."

For Virilio, the critique of speed should concentrate on his own idea of undertaking the imperative of responsibility for the generations to come. This imperative is to be taken on in line with the opening of the first Museum of Accidents, and can be defined as future-oriented critical work that speaks out against the breakdown of moral and aesthetic markers in the sense that it is not directed by the idea of a loss of meaning. Such an imperative implies that an analytical engagement with the trajective event should remain receptive to meaning instead of already being led by a conventional discourse of nihilism that is intensely meaningless (the denigration of aesthetic judgment or taste, for example) from the start. Therefore the "meaninglessness" of the "victims" is never considered. This is because the trajective event has not been explicated in terms of its "actors." Rather, the trajective event has inaugurated a sequence of potentially meaningful views and responses. Thus Virilio argues that assuming the imperative of responsibility for the generations to come is related to the idea of evading "the planetary dimensions of an integral accident," one "capable of integrating a whole heap of incidents and disasters through chain reactions" (2007a: 24). The work of the critic of speed is consequently not simply to "clarify" the trajective event of the integral accident. More readily, it is to attend to its chief actors (fanatical scientists, postmodern technicians, latter-day propagandists of progress) and to respond to it "right now" by "building, inhabiting, and thinking through the laboratory of cataclysms, the museum of the accident of technical progress." Virilio's main illustration of this process is the "accident in all knowledge, a full-scale philosophical accident which genetic engineering, in the wake of atomic engineering, now portends."

In a culture that is already steered by discourses of genetic and atomic engineering and of the modern technical beyond, the work of the critic of the art of technology is thus to reveal the tendencies inherent in trajective events. As in the "air crash" that is concealed in the discourses surrounding "the invention of the supersonic airliner," the critic of the art of technology releases them both for study (p. 5). This examination is, in its turn, critical: the work of criticism is to disclose the shock of the trajective event and not to suppress the likelihood of, say, nuclear meltdown, by describing it in terms of traditional technoscientific knowledge. In this regard, as critics of the art of technology, our efforts to undertake the imperative of responsibility for the generations to come must be concentrated on the accident and on our own future-oriented critical work. For there is no easy or fast solution to the meaninglessness of trajective events, but preferably honesty – regardless of the harm caused by outwardly blameless and "progressive" ideas such as "scientific revolution" or "ideological liberation" (p. 25). Virilio summarizes this process through a focus on the chaos caused by progress, by radio, by cinema newsreels, and particularly by television. Hence, like the undertaking of the imperative of responsibility for the generations to come, the Museum of Accidents is symbolic of our own future-oriented critical work. Evaluating trajective events in a manner that is critical of speed forever leaves them open to additional meaningful inspection and reflection instead of abandoning them to a loss of meaning and thus escalating the modern technical beyond of "flying into the unknown." This apparently inexhaustible process of revealing the Museum of Accidents is best demonstrated in media criticism. The fact that we have watched cinema does not make it anything other than "time exposing itself as the sequences scroll past." No viewing of the television set is exempt either from the speed of television's cross-frontier omnipresence or from its devastating effects on the history that is up and coming before us. Revealing the Museum of Accidents will always create additional and diverse historical thoughts and feelings for dwelling both on the Museum of Accidents that is the television set and on the world of perception. Every analysis of the Museum of Accidents will have distinct points of concentration, dispute, and influence, and therefore it will unlock potentialities for atypical yet meaningful beliefs about cinematic and televisual cultures. Cinema and television do not have clear-cut or rigid meanings, which the critic of the art of technology aspires to locate for all time. Instead, cinema and television include a huge variety of analog and now digital meanings, perceptual impressions, rhythmic inferences, and trajective events that are accessible to temporal inquiry, televisual debate, and arguments over instantaneity. Unlocking ways to undertake the imperative of responsibility for the generations to come, the discourse of the Museum of Accidents helps us to interpret any work of cinematic visual art or accelerated television imagery. For Virilio, therefore, to engage with the discourse of the Museum of Accidents and with the culture from which it and we come is to aspire to reveal trajective events, audiovisual speed, and televiewers, and to expose them all to the critique of the art of technology.

ART AS FAR AS THE EYE CAN SEE: "THE NIGHT OF THE MUSEUMS"

One of Virilio's recent books functions as a useful illustration of how he puts to work, in his own texts, the concepts of culture, the Museum of Accidents, and a critical approach to contemporary art and technology. This book, *Art as Far as the Eye Can See*, especially in the chapter "The Night of the Museums" (2007b: 69–114), considers the destiny of the art museum.

"The Night of the Museums" is a critique of France's "Museum Night," introduced in 2005 "to attract a public no longer to be seen darkening museum doors" (p. 75). Virilio's reflections look at French politics and culture through the interactions between the "open door" "operation," the "bid to win over new audiences," and the creation of "new reflexes." It is not a typical critique, though. As Virilio states, his appraisal of what is taking place here contemplates it in terms of a marketing campaign. What is of interest is not what some minister for culture pronounces, but what this "operation" signifies. This is therefore a critique of the failure "to control the intrinsic quality of artworks, contemporary or otherwise, entering the collections of French museums." It is a political critique, or rather a meditation on Virilio's unease about the plummeting of attendances, and it examines this desperate shot at novelty following the "Spring of Museums" in 1999, which attracted a million more entries. "The Night of the Museums" therefore analyzes the warning signs, "surprise attack," and trajective events within the free of charge night-time entry to over 700 museums in France from Virilio's perspective on the Museum of Accidents – a perspective that his work on the imperative of responsibility for the generations to come espouses.

From this starting point, Virilio outlines the narrative of the French night art museum from its inauguration in Paris, through its efforts to

> attract the hordes of the young and the not so young as they emerged from their nightclubs; the whole thing being graced with ambient music such as in the Musée Gustave-Moreau, where evening visitors could thrill to the rhythms of Salomé's dance. (2007b: 76)

In Virilio's writings, these developments become more than remarks about night visitors at museums of art: they are a way into various multifaceted theoretical, cultural, political, and urban difficulties liable to be confronted by the Museum of Accidents. No particular artwork appears (or is situated in the Museum of Accidents). Rather, Virilio undertakes the imperative of responsibility for the generations to come, for the trajective event of night visitors at art museums – which, in his work, generates an array of fake "art lovers" who interconnect with and interrogate diverse discourses concerning the Museum of Accidents.

"The Night of the Museums" thus concentrates unequivocally on the function of night visitors in Virilio's long-term project of setting up the Museum of Accidents. Through discussions of contemporary art and artworks and of their associations with the tide of twenty-first century thinking about night visitors, he undertakes the imperative of responsibility for the generations to come (p. 76). Furthermore, he does so through a focus on night visitors' possible effect on the Museum of Accidents, on the visible artworks, and he weighs up their potential for aesthetic and museological disturbance. In an important section he argues that the formula

"Open at Night" proclaims the estrangement of the public from the increasingly privatized art museum and from other sacred buildings:

> After the disaffection with museums, how long before we see the disaffection with places of worship that can then be turned into places of mass lay culture [. . .] [into] the hyper-realism of an art market whose by-products will finally shunt aside works of art? (2007b: 77)

This is a lucid summation of the public's break with the privatized art museum from Virilio's standpoint. Cathedrals and churches are to become sites of mass consumer culture. The public should not accept the hyperrealism of the contemporary art market or engage with that art market's spin-offs ("art" posters, postcards, DVDs, badges, pencils, and so on). Finally, it must not allow these offshoots to expel the artworks from the museum. Bill Gates, for example, the chairman of Microsoft, and playing the role of the new Howard Hughes, already owns a "dwelling of over 6,000 square metres," from where he "can call up, at every instant, displays of the works of the museums of the entire world on the multiple screens that decorate the walls of his rooms" (p. 126). The museum is then being redesigned, not by the public or by the artworks that constitute it, and certainly not by the generations to come, but by those who are literally plundering it, by those whom Virilio calls the "advocates of an audiovisual administration" and who wish to dispose of the "music of the spheres." This is what makes the work of the contemporary art museum a trajective event, and what leads the way to an analysis that aims to understand its aesthetic potential in order to defy the implicit, everyday modes of thought and behavior of a culture or discourse of noise. No actual or possible "answer" for the generations to come is offered, but the current practices of dissonance are disturbed: the shrill work of the postmodern art museum functions to suffocate the "voices of silence" at work in all museums. Consequently, the task of the critic of the art of technology and of the media theorist is to react to the smothering of those "voices of silence" in a manner that defies the "voices of the siren," which at present act to stifle their very being.

CONCLUSION

Virilio's critical writing on art and technology disturbs conventional aesthetic and technological discourses. Owing to his concentration on concepts such as the aesthetics of disappearance, the logistics of perception, the accident, and what I have called the trajective event, he does not offer a method or an agenda for media theory and practice. Rather, he advises the critic of the art of technology to probe such agendas and to examine what voices of silence they suppress.

Virilio's work therefore presents numerous possibilities for media theorists to utilize in their investigations of the museum and of the accident. It is not a question of fleeing into Bill Gates's aesthetically oriented yet ultimately dystopian electronic spectacles and manifold computer screens. Instead Virilio argues that the critic of the art of technology's work is to further the construction of the Museum of Accidents, to render the instants where the discourses that comprise the technical beyond of "flying into the unknown" are examined and where the opportunity for something other, something new, appears. His recent writings present outstanding, if difficult, explanations of these processes related to night visitors at the art museum.

CONCLUSION

Virilio's texts are having an important influence on media theory. As we saw in Chapter 1, his most powerful text, *The Aesthetics of Disappearance*, is now a benchmark for reflections on the age of the aesthetics of disappearance in philosophy and film studies, politics, new media studies, and cultural geography. No contemporary survey of aesthetics is complete without at least an allusion to that volume or his other media texts. Several of these additional media-related writings also attract more expert readers in media theory, and these, too, contest established methods in art and critical theory, technological and museum studies.

However, the issue of the degree of Virilio's impact on media theory is complicated. Because, as Chapter 5 revealed, he has not assembled a full-blown critical method that can be used to explicate aesthetic texts or cinematic events, reactions to his work are inclined to connect with his assertions and to appropriate his thoughts for application in other media, while not pursuing the broader connotations of his investigations. Yet there are growing numbers of Virilians writing in media theory now, and thus we can surely declare that his concepts are more significant and prominent. His ideas and forms of reasoning increasingly surface in a variety of diverse critical media theorists' explorations of postmodern culture, including those whose political or theoretical standpoints go against his own. Actually, those media theorists who oppose Virilio frequently offer attractive and distinctive interpretations of his writings, as we have shown in Chapter 5 with the work of the cultural geographer Nigel Thrift. Virilio's engagements with many of the key thinkers in Western continental philosophy – like Aristotle and Walter Benjamin, Gilles Deleuze, Edmund Husserl, Martin Heidegger, Maurice Merleau-Ponty, and Karl Popper – are bringing about understandings that are being taken on board by other intellectuals who have developed around those theorists, and they remain vital texts in those constituencies. Likewise, concepts such as the aesthetics of disappearance, media events, and the logistics of perception, which Virilio has discovered, reoriented, or expanded upon, often emerge in media theoretical perspectives where he is not the focus of consideration. Nevertheless, there are several major fields where his writings on the media are presently being explored and developed. These are the aesthetics of disappearance and cinema, the city, technology, museums, and accidents. All of these will be contemplated below, together with critics of the art of technology who have responded to his work in these spheres.

Since the publication of *The Aesthetics of Disappearance*, deliberations on the era of the aesthetics of disappearance have increased within media theory. Virilio's influence in this area is enormous. His description of the aesthetics of disappearance as an "irresistible project and projection toward a technical beyond" (2009a: 103) is one of the most helpful explanations of the aesthetic condition of disappearance, though it is occasionally misinterpreted or misrepresented. With Jean Baudrillard (2009), critics of the art of technology frequently quote him as an original thinker in the realm of aesthetics and disappearance within media theory. Then again, as Chapter 2 argued, Baudrillard created a very different explanation of aesthetics and disappearance, and he has inspired divergent themes of analysis and worked to different objectives (see for example Clarke, Doel, Merrin, and Smith 2008). Due to the scope and particularities of Virilio's writings on the media, it is difficult to allocate to him a precise kind of aesthetics or to restrict his impact to a specific area of disappearance. Nonetheless, I argue that those viewpoints that take the aesthetics of disappearance as a theoretical issue or as a constructive political contestation of recognized methods of elucidating media culture name him as one of their main sources of inspiration.

While countless media theorists have employed Virilio's writings on the aesthetics of disappearance, some of the most topical and important engagements with a Virilian conception of the time of the aesthetics of disappearance in the subjects of modernism and media, technology, and the philosophy of film incorporate the texts below. An excellent discussion of the aesthetics of disappearance, postmodern culture, and advertising can be found in Ryan Bishop and John Phillips's *Modernist Avant-Garde Aesthetics and Contemporary Military Technology* (2010: 63), which is set to become one of the paradigm studies of the epoch of the aesthetics of disappearance, and its appraisals of Virilio are extremely creative. The authors regard the aesthetics of disappearance as more than simply a modernist avant-garde phenomenon, exposing contemporary advertising from the Boeing Corporation to the actual instance of its Comanche helicopter to examine the changes that have occurred in our sense and awareness of aesthetics and speed throughout the present period, and the outcome of these transformations on how we experience technology and imagery. Referring to many more of Virilio's texts than *The Aesthetics of Disappearance* (and in an incredibly productive way), their scrutiny of the aesthetics of disappearance bears a similarity to Virilio's study of the discourses of history and speed in *The Aesthetics of Disappearance* and can be read together with that text.

For readers fascinated by perception and by the medium of cinema, an outstanding discussion that uses the writings of Virilio to question conventional practices of analyzing warfare is Friedrich Kittler's *Optical Media* (2010). For Kittler, the concept of war must be appreciated in a dual sense: not only does the bomb over Hiroshima indicate the beginning of atomic warfare as a modern technical beyond of hyper-Virilian proportions, but it also initiates a study of conflict as has never been attempted before, given that Kittler examines it through his inquiry into representations and photographic flashes, annihilations, war plans, military images, and bomb-proof shelters. Virilio is an important point of departure for this calling into question of conventional academic models of combat, and Kittler's evaluation of *War and Cinema: The Logistics of Perception* is not only a useful introduction to ideas such as those expressed by Virilio in *The Information Bomb* (2000d), but also a valuable manifestation of the exception that his writings take to traditional military strategy.

In English literary criticism and the philosophy of film there are varied endeavors to develop Virilio's concepts. One of the most accomplished theorists in this effort, and undoubtedly one of the most valuable for researchers into postmodern technology, literature, and media culture, is the British critic Alex Goody, whose *Technology, Literature, and Culture* (2011) offers analyses of a vast array of visual technologies and modern warfare in historical literature and culture, regarding many of Virilio's notions around the age of the aesthetics of disappearance and the convergence of media and military technologies. Instead of offering a study of Virilio's writings on the Gulf War and the like, Goody concentrates on the changes that have occurred in literature and in the cultures of military technology since the nineteenth century (thus portraying "technology as a generative force in culture, often tied in closely to the military," in a way Virilio would), in order to offer a succession of examinations of the materiality of technology's ability to connect with wider questions of interpretation and representation. A crucial feature of Goody's book is its author's deliberation on the social meanings and politics of technology and on their association with contemporary attempts made by critics of the art of technology to modify and question existing literary conceptions of technology; and she embraces Virilio's work on the media as a major constituent of her critical standpoint on this issue. Another significant analysis of Virilio's writings within the philosophy of film is the Dutch media theorist Patricia Pister's multifaceted article "Logistics of Perception 2.0: Multiple Screen Aesthetics in Iraq War Films" (2010), which considers Virilio's importance for postmodern film theory about the Iraq War.

One other subject where Virilio's writings on the media are prominent is the city. There is a growing interest in the connections between the city and its future in media theory, and an increasing body of research on what it means to be in the city in the postmodern globalized world inquires into the modern concept of the city. Many of these writings employ Virilio's explorations of the cultural politics of the city, especially in *A Landscape of Events* and in *City of Panic*, in order to rethink the boundaries of the city as it exists in contemporary media culture. As Chapters 3, 4, and 5 argued,

Virilio's critical new media theory questions the city through his ideas of vision and inertia, of the accident, of panic, of the instrumental image loop of television, of theatrical militarism, of visual discourses of distraction, and of media events. Furthermore, this critique of the technologies of the art of vision has been adopted more recently by Virilio himself and by many other media theorists as a way of undertaking the imperative of responsibility for the generations to come and of considering the effects that events relating to general mobilization and the advent of heavily armed terrorists have had on our awareness of what it means to be in the city in the twenty-first century.

A clear introduction to Virilio's most recent writings on the city is a brief chapter by Virilio himself, titled "The Ultracity," in his book *The Futurism of the Instant: Stop–Eject* (2010b: 32–69). This piece understands the "ultracity" and the putting of gigantic masses of people in motion in contemporary civilization in relation to other media theorists' examinations of the "Reign of Quantity," the "bulk carrier revolution," and the "imminent mutation of just-in-time distribution systems" that were "supposed to achieve the instant globalization of profit" (pp. 32–3). For Virilio, René Guénon's arguments, in *The Crisis of the Modern World* (2002), about the infringement of "the capacity of the 'transport revolution'" into all facets of existence and about the simultaneous mobilization of "the mass of civilian populations" provide a springboard from which we can appreciate the influence of the growth of geographical exodus, political exile, and deportation – for instance, France's massive deportation of the Romanian and Bulgarian Roma, in an onslaught on "illegal camps" in the country (see Armitage 2010: 18–19). Virilio's evaluation of Guénon is shrewd, and *The Futurism of the Instant* develops his subject of study, which is fast increasing in significance in media theory.

A multifaceted and philosophically exploratory deliberation is presented in a chapter by Arthur Kroker in my edited book *Virilio Now: Current Perspectives in Virilio Studies* (2011: 158–76). These captivating "Three Theses on Virilio Now" make use of Virilio's writings to understand the links between the city, transformation, and US President Barack Obama's America. Virilio's media and political theory are touched upon throughout the chapter – which also includes a perceptive analysis of his writings on simulation and disturbance, Walter Benjamin, the eye, and signs (from *City of Panic*). What Kroker (2011: 158) signals here is the import, for postmodern media culture, history, and criticism, of Virilio's awareness of the city, of that which, within the city, opposes "these twilight times in which we live" either to the aestheticized disappearance of the city or to the innumerable informational, military, and media systems that have come to displace it. One valuable compilation of Virilio's essays, which also contend with Virilio's media theory of speed and comprise "The Insecurity of History" and "Too Late for Private Life," is *The Great Accelerator* (2012). This volume gathers Virilio's latest major contributions to this field of analysis and considers them with clarity.

In view of Virilio's studies of technology, museums, and the accident, which we have discussed throughout this volume, it is also important to identify these subjects as ones where his writings continue to expand. There is a rising concern with the technological, museological, and political significance of the accident, and Virilio's writings here are highly influential: technology has, in recent times, become the crucial category of critical inquiry, and his understandings of the status of technology in aesthetics and cinema, war, new media, vision, inertia, the city, television, media events, art, and in the museum are major points of orientation for those delving into the political, theoretical, and practical effects of this concept within postmodern media culture.

The main volume for feminist researchers surveying Virilio's influence on these postmodern discussions of technology is *Fast Feminism* (2010) by Shannon Bell. This text scrutinizes how Virilio's idea of technological speed induces Bell's analyses of a new feminism grounded in politics; and her examinations of performance and Virilian philosophy create vital advances in his theories, poststructuralism, and "cyberfeminism 3.0." Constructively, Bell associates Virilio's writings not merely with contemporary fast philosophers and feminist critics of the art of technology, but also with various other key current theories, queer theory and queer politics, to give a feeling for the variety of postmodern philosophical interest in an oppositional relationship to dominant technological values.

A significant article by a contemporary British sociologist is Nick Prior's "Speed, Rhythm and Time–Space: Museums and Cities" (2011: 197–213). This article employs Virilio's writings, for instance *The Vision Machine*, and also Henri Lefebvre's (2004) *Rhythmanalysis: Space, Time, and Everyday Life*, to explore the meaning of the museum for the history of the city, and also for the theory of modernity and speed. It offers an incisive analysis of where the critique of the art of speed, time, and space is headed, and also of Virilio's significance for this museological and urban development.

Recently, Virilio's critique of the art of technology has increasingly emphasized the importance of the accident. Major publications in this emergent area are his *The University of Disaster* (2010a: 15) and *The Great Accelerator* (2012). The former deals with the growth of "the risk of an accident in knowledge" from the twentieth century until today, and its analyses of the accident "in the near future, only add to the accident in the substances of an ecology that takes seriously Aristotle's second axiom: 'Completion is a limit.'" Virilio looks at the politics of differing conceptions of the accident, from the "local accident" to the "integral accident," arguing that the accident in knowledge appears "when catastrophe turns into a system" and yet is also able to bring about the means to assess an "ecosystem" of catastrophe that is no longer separate but connected. "The Accident of Finance" (2011: 177–99) by Paul Crosthwaite, in *Virilio Now*, also examines the importance of a deliberation on the accident in knowledge for literary and media cultural criticism. However, Crosthwaite is much more optimistic than Virilio about the likelihood of hitting upon resolutions of the dangers to the lifestyles of people across the world, notwithstanding the (apparently) increasingly recurring financial failures of global stock markets. In Crosthwaite's chapter, though, the accident is employed as a way to broach questions concerning the architectural, informational, and socio-economic organizational systems of the post-nuclear planet Earth, and his method of interrogating the diverse interpretations of the accident bear many comparisons with Virilio's idea of undertaking the imperative of responsibility for the generations to come, which was presented in Chapter 5.

Virilio's significance continues to increase as critics of the art of technology revisit, time and again, his writings on the media to discover new techniques for grasping the intricate and urgent tribulations that confront postmodern media culture. As his writings are increasingly and ever more rapidly translated into English, the issues he engages with are larger, and the influence of his critical studies on aesthetics and cinema, new media, the city, the art of technology, and the Museum of Accidents is growing within media theory. The degree of Virilio's impact is somewhat uncertain, as are the directions into which critics of the art of technology will take his multipurpose media theory. Nevertheless, what is certain is that the questions posed by his theories will continue to be crucially significant for appreciating the world of contemporary media in the foreseeable future.

GUIDE TO FURTHER READING

WORKS BY PAUL VIRILIO

All of Virilio's media-related texts considered in *Virilio and the Media* are obtainable in English. Most readers initially encounter his theoretical concepts regarding the media through books such as *The Aesthetics of Disappearance* or *War and Cinema*. These are the best books to garner an impression of his critique of the art of technology and media theory, but they are not typical of its full extent. *The Vision Machine*, for example, develops the questions posed in those two texts, while *Polar Inertia* affords a route into his work on new media in *The Art of the Motor* and in *Open Sky*. Some readers will want to investigate his previous writings that are not concerned with media, for instance *Speed and Politics: An Essay on Dromology* or *Popular Defense and Ecological Struggles*. These are complex books, but ones that are nevertheless captivating and the center of rising theoretical attention. Readers may also be attracted by his photographic or shorter critical articles originally published in European newspapers and periodicals, which appear in *Bunker Archeology* and *Strategy of Deception*, *A Landscape of Events*, *The Information Bomb*, and *Desert Screen*. Each of these books includes selections from his works on the subjects we have deliberated on in this book. Further details of the ten key Virilio media-related texts are provided below.

Virilio and the Media has concentrated on the principal media-related texts by Virilio from 1980 to 2012, which we can label his "aesthetic" writings, centered as they are on the concept of disappearance. However, there are other significant works, for instance *The Lost Dimension*, *Ground Zero*, *Unknown Quantity*, and *Negative Horizon*, which could not be considered fully here for lack of room. Even so, the main books, such as *Art and Fear*, *City of Panic*, *The Original Accident*, and *Art as Far as the Eye Can See* are listed underneath, with accounts of their subject matter, import, and reader-friendliness.

In this section Virilio's media-related writings are arranged by their earliest publication date, to offer an outline of his publishing history. All of the works listed were originally published in French. The publication particulars specify the English translations. Consequently, two dates are to be found in the references: the first, in square brackets, is the date of the original French publication, while the second date and all further information relate to the translation.

[1980] (2009) *The Aesthetics of Disappearance*, trans. P. Beitchman. New York: Semiotext(e).
This is Virilio's first and most important book on media theory. It reflects on the importance of the aesthetics of disappearance and on the varieties of picnolepsy, on the state of human consciousness and on speed, subjectivity, absence, and cinema.

[1984] (1989) *War and Cinema: The Logistics of Perception*, trans. P. Camiller. London: Verso.
This is Virilio's main work on synchronized camera/machine guns. It is a multifaceted but inspiring text, which offers intriguing reflections on aircraft and war, computing, and the technologies of cinema.

[1988] (1994) *The Vision Machine*, trans. J. Rose. London: British Film Institute.
The Vision Machine examines the technologies of perception, production, and the historical development and proliferation of images. Writing as an art historian and focusing on the technologies of war and urban planning, Virilio employs concepts coined in *War and Cinema* and *The Aesthetics of Disappearance* to demonstrate the problems that this new "logistics of the image" raises for postmodern media theory and culture.

[1990] (2000) *Polar Inertia*, trans. P. Camiller. London: Sage.
This book is a critical analysis of the relationships between space and time, and it remains Virilio's most comprehensive text on how the "here and now" of place, territory, and the body are being reorganized by new technologies. Inertia as the crucial state of contemporary culture is the main thesis.

[1995] (1997) *Open Sky*, trans. J. Rose. London: Verso.
This is an important text, which we surveyed in Chapter 3. Originally published in French two years after *The Art of the Motor* (1993), it is a book about time, perspective, and whether it is feasible to have practical notions of real time and optics, imme-

diacy, and ecology in the age of the aesthetics of disappearance.

[1997] (2000) *A Landscape of Events*, trans. J. Rose. Cambridge, MA: The MIT Press.
This is Virilio's important and sweeping book on the cultural pandemonium of the late twentieth century. In it he anticipates his thoughts on urban terror, presented in *City of Panic* and *The Original Accident*, to create a resourceful viewpoint on techno-warfare and the acceleration of events.

[2000] (2003) *Art and Fear*, trans. J. Rose. London: Continuum.
This book is the product of two lectures where Virilio critiques art, technology, and the mass media through his discussion of the postmodern phenomenon of "pitiless art." It also incorporates the lecture "Silence on Trial," wherein he separates himself from "the age of the sonorization of images and all audiovisual icons" (p. 69).

[2004] (2005) *City of Panic*, trans. J. Rose. Oxford: Berg.
In his inquiry into the city, Virilio reflects on panic and on terrified and conflict-ridden cities as diverse as New York, Baghdad, and Beijing. *City of Panic* also reveals the rapid transformations in his work when contrasted with *Polar Inertia* and *A Landscape of Events*.

[2005] (2007) *The Original Accident*, trans. J. Rose. Cambridge: Polity.
This compilation of Virilio's essays is an important contribution to the debate that was engendered by

his 2002–3 art exhibition *Ce qui arrive*. The essays offer linkages between *Ce qui arrive* and *Art and Fear*, and they amplify his ideas regarding the invention of accidents and museums, the synchronization of emotions, and widespread acceleration.

[2005] (2007) *Art as Far as the Eye Can See*, trans. J. Rose. Oxford: Berg.

This book concentrates on important philosophical topics in Virilio's theory of the media: the event, art, museums, and perception. Considering his position on aesthetics, looking, and politics in texts such as *The Aesthetics of Disappearance*, he contests new media art and technology, speed, and mass culture.

WORKS ON AND INTERVIEWS WITH PAUL VIRILIO

Virilio and the Media is the most straightforward critical introduction to Virilio's writings on the media. For readers wanting to consider stages of Virilio's work or to concentrate on his interviews, the following texts, listed in alphabetical author–date order, are the places to start. Due to the contentious nature of Virilio's writings, critics often take a position regarding his work. Generally, those supportive of Virilio would take in most of the authors below, while those who contest at least some of his claims might incorporate Adam Sharr, Elin O'Hara Slavick, and Nigel Thrift in *Virilio Now*, and, at least concerning Virilio's writings on the aesthetics of disappearance, Sean Cubitt in the same volume. The comments below provide information about the focal points and degree of difficulty of the texts.

Armitage, J. (ed.) (2000) *Paul Virilio: From Modernism to Hypermodernism and Beyond*. London: Sage.
This is an outstanding anthology of essays, which includes a long interview with Virilio; the essays are authored by British, American, and Australian theorists and they deal with his cultural work – especially with *Polar Inertia*, architecture, bunkers, war, and technology. While philosophically complex, the chapters present Virilio's contentions regarding his critiques of new media and speed, accidents, feminism, and society.

Armitage, J. (ed.) (2001) *Virilio Live: Selected Interviews*. London: Sage.
This is an exceptional introduction to Virilio's writings through significant interviews. Virilio talks eloquently, while elaborating on the details of his claims related to media theory and culture, society, architecture, speed, space, politics, art, technology, the integral accident, and military strategy.

Armitage, J. (ed.) (2011) *Virilio Now: Current Perspectives in Virilio Studies*. Cambridge: Polity.
These original essays concentrate on Virilio's important challenges to war and the city, contemporary art, and architecture. The book provides a critical overview of his work to date and presents supportive yet also critical assessments of it as to politics and the aesthetics of disappearance, media, philosophy, the accident, and visual culture, concluding with Virilio's own considerations on postmodern advertising.

Brausch, M. and Virilio, P. (2011) *A Winter's Journey: Four Conversations with Marianne Brausch*. Chicago: University of Chicago Press.
This book consists of four interviews with Virilio, and one of them probes the importance of his arguments pertaining

to architecture. Most helpful is the examination of Virilio's existing writings on twenty-first-century technological acceleration and of his emphasis on technocultural accidents and brutality, war, space, militarization, events, culture, and theories of contemporary civilization.

Der Derian, J. (ed.) (1998) *The Virilio Reader*. Oxford: Blackwell.
This book contemplates the meaning of the military in Virilio's work. *The Virilio Reader* discusses "military space" and "the suicidal state" as well as "the state of emergency," and it concentrates on ideas developed in *The Lost Dimension*, *War and Cinema*, and *Polar Inertia*. Virilio's writings offer revelations on all these and numerous other texts such as *The Vision Machine*, *The Art of the Motor*, *Desert Screen*, and *Open Sky*.

James, I. (2007) *Paul Virilio*. London: Routledge.
This first-rate presentation introduces the reader to Virilio's critical political philosophy of perception and discusses how he has developed his postmodern thinking on speed and virtualization. The chapters on Virilio's conceptions of war, politics, and art provide deliberations on *War and Cinema*, *Speed and Politics*, and *Art and Fear*, in addition to comments on his work on the insecurity of territory and the history of vision.

Lotringer, S. and Virilio, P. (2005) *The Accident of Art*. New York, Semiotext(e).
This is a high-quality introduction to the scope of Virilio's thinking on the accident and on art that, while deriving from a series of interviews that are occasionally complex, employs various examples from art to show the influence of such vital notions as pitiless art, the accident of art, and the Museum

of Accidents. Lotringer's use of the interview form, which draws on instances taken from terrorism, vision, and technology, makes this an appealing book about Virilio's aesthetic philosophy of accidents and museums.

Petit, P. and Virilio, P. (1999) *The Politics of the Very Worst*. New York: Semiotext(e).

This is a short book of interviews that explore Virilio's questioning of the transportation and communications revolutions. Although it makes use of Virilio's arguments in *Negative Horizon* and *The Vision Machine*, it also offers an introduction to his aesthetics of disappearance and war, perception, and politics in postmodern culture.

Redhead, S. (2004) *Paul Virilio: Theorist for an Accelerated Culture*. Edinburgh: Edinburgh University Press.

This introduction sketches Virilio's ideas from his early works up to *Art and Fear* and offers a distinctive reading of the main texts. Redhead interprets Virilio from the perspective of modernity rather than from that of media theory, which gives his study a different intonation from the one to be found in *Virilio and the Media*.

Virilio, P. and Lotringer, S. (2008) *Pure War*, New York: Semiotext(e).

This is the most clear-cut introduction to Virilio's writings, and it is a first-rate next stage for readers intending to discover more concerning the shift from his works on war to his philosophy of speed and space. Lotringer's book-length interview outlines the development of Virilio's writings and offers crucial insights into his theory of technology and its relations with politics, the military, movement, and cinema.

GLOSSARY

This non-technical glossary is an alphabetical list of concepts regarding those aspects of Virilio's media theory that are discussed in this book. All the examples are taken from Virilio's texts. It is a short dictionary offered to readers as an aide-memoire concerning the approximate meanings of Virilio's important media-related ideas. The glossary aims to be neither theoretically comprehensive nor meticulously authoritative.

Accident An unlucky event that occurs without warning and inadvertently, characteristically producing destruction or wounding, for example a collision involving automobiles, people, fatalities, and/or acute and minor injuries.

Accident in Knowledge That contemporary form of belief in the virtualization of the real world and in the obliteration of accumulated human knowledge, including that of the university. The accident in knowledge is due to the "success" of various experiments made by technoscientists with bio- and nanotechnologies and will possibly initiate the annihilation of all life on Earth.

Aesthetics of Disappearance The mediated technological effects typical of the contemporary arts. Whereas the ancient aesthetics of appearance was based on lasting material supports (wood/canvas in the case of paintings; marble in the case of statues, and so on), the present-day aesthetics of disappearance is founded on temporary immaterial supports (e.g. plastic/digital storage in the case of films). Contemporary images therefore do not so much appear (except as a function of human cognition) as they continually disappear. Postmodern images apparently move across, but actually they vanish repeatedly from the fundamentally immaterial support of the screen, as part of a cinematic sequence. In the case of film, such images disappear at 24 frames per second or, in the case of special effects, at 60 frames per second and above.

A Landscape of Events A contemporary scene where the significant occurrence is that of cultural disorder, a disorder that simultaneously signals both the brutality and the bewilderment of our era and corresponds to our everyday lives and behavior in the midst of cities seemingly ever more overflowing with freely available weaponry. Unending war, the speeding up of reality, and frantic media reporting of mounting anarchy all contribute to the landscape of events – for instance on August 30, 1985, when a drug dealer is interrogated by police in the Place des Innocents, Paris, and there is an uprising immediately afterwards.

Instrumental Image Loop of Television That instrumental image instantaneously and increasingly supplied for television audiences on the basis of repetition. The instrumental "image loop" is the televisual signature of contemporary catastrophes; such is the image, instantly shown to TV audiences and continuously repeated, of the "live" re-entry breakup over Texas of *Space Shuttle Columbia* on February 1, 2003, which, on its 28th mission, killed all seven crew members.

Integral Accident The accident that might become our only habitat after the chaos inflicted by "progress." The integral accident will expand to the totality of world geophysical space and to the duration of centuries.

Local Accident An accident that is exactly located in space and time, such as the sinking of the RMS *Titanic* at 02.20 a.m. on April 15, 1912, 400 miles south of the Grand Banks of Newfoundland in the North Atlantic.

Logistics of Perception The military provision of imagery that, from World War I (1914–18) onwards, developed into a counterpart to the military provision of ammunition, thus establishing a new, cinematic weapons system, derived from the amalgamation of means of war transportation and cameras.

Media Event An occasion, planned or unplanned, that attracts extensive reporting by mass media organizations, chiefly television news; an example would be the killing, recorded on September 30, 2000 by Talal Abu Rahma, a freelance Palestinian cameraman working for *France 2*, of the 12-year-old Palestinian boy Muhammad Jamal al-Durrah, allegedly murdered by the Israeli Defense Forces during a gunfire clash with Palestinian Security Forces in the Gaza Strip.

Museum of Accidents A museum, as yet unrealized, proposed by Virilio to counter the breakdown of moral and artistic markers, the loss of values people observe as casualties of the outrages perpetrated by the mass media, and the intensification of people's sense of imminent tragedy. The Museum of Accidents therefore raises questions regarding the unforeseen, one's inattentiveness to major risks, and the need for "preventive intelligence."

Picnolepsy A recurrent yet brief deficiency in visual sense performance, in which consciousness of the outside world is impeded but reappears abruptly; the state involves a momentary interruption of vision, speech, and action and its being triggered back to awareness. However, following the interruption, consciousness and time combine again instinctively, producing an ostensibly uninterrupted time. Such interruptions happen repeatedly each day, habitually passing by unobserved either by the "picnoleptic" or by others as, for both, nothing occurred, the absent time never existed. Yet each interruption signals that a minute fraction of the picnoleptic's existence has disappeared.

Polar Inertia A state or "location" in which or where people cease to be moving bodies and become instead motionless, where everything happens "on the spot," in the immediacy of an action that abolishes spatial extension and prolonged time periods – as when people abandon bicycling along roads and turn to the stationary "exercise bike" as a substitute, where space no longer unfolds in front of them and the instant of inertia replaces constant bodily movement.

Statistical Imagery Artificial images that can only appear through the fast computation, deciphering, and analysis of the pixels a computer graphics system can show on a screen. Such images create "rational" visual illusions that damage people's comprehension as well as their ability to interpret the real world.

Synchronization of Emotions The idea that television, which increasingly lets millions of people observe the same event at the same time, has become a theatrical performance. Politics, for example, has become part of the entertainment industry, where it is the emotional performance that convinces audiences of the opinion that the candidate, perhaps United States President Barack Obama, is genuine. Here, sustaining the delusion or synchronizing the theatrical production being presented to the audience is the "tele-objective" of contemporary mass media.

Technical Beyond The West's distinctive, compulsive scheme and projection toward specific aesthetic techniques at or to the further side of the theoretical threshold and/or practical scope of contemporary culture; an enigmatic desire for a technological "elsewhere" or quasi-religious understanding of technology derived from cinematic special effects and/or the fantasies produced for television by props, camerawork, and computer graphics, etc.

Technical Prostheses of Subliminal Comfort Artificial additions related to cultural technologies, particularly additions to the human eye – such as cameras or other apparatuses for taking photographs or for making films or television programs – made for the express purpose of arousing and accelerating mental processes below the threshold of sensation or consciousness; the use of such cultural technologies and artificial additions as forms of perception that influence people's minds without those people being conscious of it and in a state of physical relaxation and freedom from pain or restraint.

Theatrical Militarism Deception in the military "theater of operations," as in the US military assault on Baghdad during the Iraq War (begun on March 3, 2003), which concluded in the histrionically staged destruction, for global television audiences, of the statue of then Iraqi President Saddam Hussein in Fardus Square.

Universal Remote Control Space That temporal–spatial condition where, as the rate of informational transfer into the real time of computerized interactivity accelerates, the more universal remote control becomes totalized, ubiquitous, and gradually displaces both the natural environment and the real space of human activity.

Visual Discourses of Distraction The televisual and military-directed organization of communications concerning, for example, turning the attention of global television audiences away from the "War on Terrorism" and toward the war on Iraq.

REFERENCES

Almond, Ian (2009) "Baudrillard's Gulf War: Saddam the Carpet-Seller," *International Journal of Baudrillard Studies* 6 (2): 1–9.

Aristotle (1998) *The Metaphysics*. London: Penguin.

Armitage, John (ed.) (2000) *Paul Virilio: From Modernism to Hypermodernism and Beyond*. London: Sage.

Armitage, John (ed.) (2001) *Virilio Live: Selected Interviews*. London: Sage.

Armitage, John (2010) "Temporary Authoritarian Zone," in Monica Narula, Shuddhabrata Sengupta, and Jeebesh Bagchi (eds.), *Sarai Reader 08: Fear*. New Delhi: Center for the Study of Developing Societies, pp. 18–19.

Armitage, John (ed.) (2011) *Virilio Now: Current Perspectives in Virilio Studies*. Cambridge: Polity.

Armitage, John and Garnett, Joy (2011) "Apocalypse Now: An Interview with Joy Garnett," *Cultural Politics* 7 (2): 59–78.

Barrett, Jennifer (2010) *Museums and the Public Sphere*. Oxford: Blackwell.

Baudrillard, Jean (1995) *The Gulf War Did Not Take Place*, trans. Paul Patton. Sydney: Power Publications.

Baudrillard, Jean (2000) "The Evil Demon of Images," in Clive Cazeaux (ed.), *The Continental Aesthetics Reader*. London: Routledge, pp. 444–52.

Baudrillard, Jean (2005) *The Intelligence of Evil or the Lucidity Pact*, trans. Chris Turner. Oxford: Berg.

Baudrillard, Jean (2009) *Why Hasn't Everything Disappeared?*, trans. Chris Turner. London: Seagull Books.

Bell, Shannon (2010) *Fast Feminism*. New York: Autonomedia.

Benjamin, Walter (1968) "The Work of Art in the Age of Mechanical Reproduction," in Walter Benjamin, *Illuminations*. New York: Schocken Books, pp. 217–51.

Bishop, Ryan and Phillips, John (2010) *Modernist Avant-Garde Aesthetics and Contemporary Military Technology*. Edinburgh: Edinburgh University Press.

Boswell, David and Evans, Jessica (eds.) (1999) *Representing the Nation: A Reader in Heritage and Museums*. London: Routledge.

Brausch, Marianne and Virilio, Paul (2011) *A Winter's Journey: Four Conversations with Marianne Brausch*, trans. Chris Turner. Chicago: University of Chicago Press.

Burroughs, William (1968) *The Ticket That Exploded*. London: Flamingo.

Carbonell, Bettina (2003) *Museum Studies: An Anthology of Contexts*. Oxford: Blackwell.

Castells, Manuel (2000) *The Rise of the Network Society*. Oxford: Blackwell.

Castells, Manuel (2009) *Communication Power*. Oxford: Blackwell.

Chomsky, Noam (1999) *The New Military Humanism: Lessons from Kosovo*. London: Pluto.

Clarke, David, Doel, Marcus, Merrin, William, and Smith, Richard G. (eds.) (2008) *Jean Baudrillard: Fatal Theories*. London: Routledge.

Coulter, Gerry (2010) "Jean Baudrillard and Cinema: The Problems of Technology, Realism and History," *Film–Philosophy* 14 (2): 6–20.

Crosthwaite, Paul (2011) "The Accident of Finance," in John Armitage (ed.), *Virilio Now: Current Perspectives in Virilio Studies*. Cambridge: Polity, pp. 177–99.

Cubitt, Sean (2001) *Simulation and Social Theory*. London: Sage.

Cubitt, Sean (2011) "Vector Politics and the Aesthetics of Disappearance," in John Armitage (ed.), *Virilio Now: Current Perspectives in Virilio Studies*. Cambridge: Polity, pp. 68–91.

Deleuze, Gilles (1995) "Postscript on Control Societies," in Gilles Deleuze, *Negotiations*. New York: Columbia University Press, pp. 177–82.

Deleuze, Gilles (2001) *Cinema 1: The Movement Image*. London: Continuum.

Deleuze, Gilles (2005) *Cinema 2: The Time Image*. London: Continuum.

Der Derian, James (ed.) (1998) *The Virilio Reader*. Oxford: Blackwell.

Eagleton, Terry (1990) *The Ideology of the Aesthetic*. Oxford: Blackwell.

Foster, Hal (ed.) (1994) *The Anti-Aesthetic: Essays on Postmodern Culture*, Seattle: Bay Press.

Friedberg, Anne (2006) *The Virtual Window: From Alberti to Microsoft*. Cambridge, MA: The MIT Press.

Gane, Mike (2000) *Jean Baudrillard: In Radical Uncertainty*. London: Pluto.

Goody, Alex (2011) *Technology, Literature, and Culture*. Cambridge: Polity.

Grace, Victoria (2008) "Baudrillard's Illusions: The Seduction of Feminism," *French Cultural Studies* 19 (3): 347–61.

Guénon, René (2002) *The Crisis of the Modern World.* Varanasi: Indica Books.

Harris, Jonathan (2006) *Art History: The Key Concepts.* London: Routledge.

Harvey, David (1991) *The Condition of Postmodernity: An Enquiry into the Origins of Cultural Change.* Oxford: Blackwell.

Heidegger, Martin (1978) "The Question Concerning Technology," in David Farrell Krell (ed.), *Martin Heidegger: Basic Writings.* London: Routledge, pp. 307–42.

James, Ian (2007) *Paul Virilio.* London: Routledge.

Jameson, Fredric (1991) *Postmodernism, or, The Cultural Logic of Late Capitalism.* London: Verso.

Jencks, Charles (2007) *Critical Modernism: Where is Post-Modernism Going? What is Post-Modernism?* Oxford: John Wiley & Sons.

Kahn, Herman (2010) *On Escalation: Metaphors and Scenarios.* New Brunswick: Transaction Publishers.

Kittler, Friedrich A. (2010) *Optical Media,* trans. Anthony Enns. Cambridge: Polity.

Kroker, Arthur (2011) "Three Theses on Virilio Now," in John Armitage (ed.), *Virilio Now: Current Perspectives in Virilio Studies.* Cambridge: Polity, pp. 158–76.

Le Gates, Richard and Stout, Frederic (eds.) (1996) *The City Reader.* London: Routledge.

Lefebvre, Henri (2004) *Rhythmanalysis: Space, Time and Everyday Life,* trans. Stuart Elden. London: Continuum.

Lipovetsky, Gilles (2005) *Hypermodern Times,* trans. Andrew Brown. Cambridge: Polity.

Lotringer, Sylvère and Virilio, Paul (2005) *The Accident of Art,* trans. Michael Taormina. New York: Semiotext(e).

Lynch, Kevin A. (1960) *The Image of the City*. Cambridge, MA: The MIT Press.

Lyon, David (1999) *Postmodernity*. Milton Keynes: Open University Press.

Lyotard, Jean-François (1984) *The Postmodern Condition: A Report on Knowledge*, trans. Geoff Bennington and Brian Massumi. Manchester: Manchester University Press.

Macdonald, Sharon (ed.) (2010) *A Companion to Museum Studies*. Oxford: Blackwell.

Merleau-Ponty, Maurice (1968) *The Visible and the Invisible*, trans. Alphonso Lingis. Evanston, IL: Northwestern University Press.

Nicholls, Peter (1995) *Modernisms: A Literary Guide*. London: Macmillan.

Petit, Philippe and Virilio, Paul (1999) *The Politics of the Very Worst*, trans. Michael Cavalière. New York: Semiotext(e).

Pisters, Patricia (2010) "Logistics of Perception 2.0: Multiple Screen Aesthetics in Iraq War Films," *Film-Philosophy* 14 (1): 232–52.

Popper, Karl (1990) *A World of Propensities*. Bristol: Thoemmes.

Prior, Nick (2011) "Speed, Rhythm, and Time–Space: Museums and Cities," *Space and Culture* 14 (2): 197–213.

Redhead, Steve (2004) *Paul Virilio: Theorist for an Accelerated Culture*. Edinburgh: Edinburgh University Press.

Rush, Michael (2005) *New Media in Art*. London: Thames and Hudson.

Sassen, Saskia (2001) *The Global City: New York, London, Tokyo*. Princeton: Princeton University Press.

Sennett, Richard (2003) *Flesh and Stone: The Body and the City in Western Civilization*. London: Penguin.

Shaw, Debra Benita (2008) *Technoculture*. Oxford: Berg.

Simmel, Georg (1969) "The Metropolis and Mental Life," in

Richard Sennett (ed.), *Classic Essays on the Culture of Cities*. Englewood Cliffs, NJ: Prentice Hall, pp. 47–60.

Stiegler, Bernard (2010) "Telecracy against Democracy," *Cultural Politics* 6 (2): 171–80.

Svendsen, Lars (2008) *A Philosophy of Fear*. London: Reaktion Books.

Tegel, Susan (2007) *Nazis and the Cinema*. London: Hambledon Continuum.

Thrift, Nigel (2011) "Panicsville: Paul Virilio and the Aesthetic of Disaster," in John Armitage (ed.), *Virilio Now: Current Perspectives in Virilio Studies*. Cambridge: Polity, pp. 145–57.

Toffoletti, Kim and Grace, Victoria (2010) "Terminal Indifference: The Hollywood War Film Post-September 11," *Film-Philosophy* 14 (2): 62–83.

Virilio, Paul (1976) *L'Insécurité du territoire*. Paris: Stock.

Virilio, Paul (2006) *Speed and Politics: An Essay on Dromology* [1986], trans. Mark Polizzotti. New York: Semiotext(e).

Virilio, Paul (1989) *War and Cinema: The Logistics of Perception*, trans. Patrick Camiller. London: Verso.

Virilio, Paul (1990) *Popular Defense and Ecological Struggles*, trans. Mark Polizzotti. New York: Semiotext(e).

Virilio, Paul (1991) *The Lost Dimension*, trans. Daniel Moshenberg. New York: Semiotext(e).

Virilio, Paul (1994a) *Bunker Archeology*, trans. George Collins. Princeton: Princeton Architectural Press.

Virilio, Paul (1994b) *The Vision Machine*, trans. Julie Rose. London: British Film Institute.

Virilio, Paul (1995) *The Art of the Motor*, trans. Julie Rose. Minneapolis: University of Minnesota Press.

Virilio, Paul (1997) *Open Sky*, trans. Julie Rose. London: Verso.

Virilio, Paul (2000a) *Polar Inertia*, trans. Patrick Camiller. London: Sage.

Virilio, Paul (2000b) *Strategy of Deception*, trans. Chris Turner. London: Verso.

Virilio, Paul (2000c) *A Landscape of Events*, trans. Julie Rose. Princeton: Princeton Architectural Press.

Virilio, Paul (2000d) *The Information Bomb*, trans. Chris Turner. London: Verso.

Virilio, Paul (2002a) *Desert Screen: War at the Speed of Light*, trans. Michael Degener. London: Continuum.

Virilio, Paul (2002b) *Ground Zero*, trans. Chris Turner. London: Verso.

Virilio, Paul (2003a) *Art and Fear*, trans. Julie Rose. London: Continuum.

Virilio, Paul (2003b) *Unknown Quantity*, trans. Chris Turner and Jian-Xing Too. London: Thames and Hudson.

Virilio, Paul (2005a) *Negative Horizon*, trans. Michel Degener. London: Continuum.

Virilio, Paul (2005b) *City of Panic*, trans. Julie Rose. Oxford: Berg.

Virilio, Paul (2007a) *The Original Accident*, trans. Julie Rose. Cambridge: Polity.

Virilio, Paul (2007b) *Art As Far As the Eye Can See*, trans. Julie Rose. Oxford: Berg.

Virilio, Paul (2009a) *The Aesthetics of Disappearance*, trans. Philip Beitchman. New York: Semiotext(e).

Virilio, Paul (2009b) *Grey Ecology*, trans. Drew Burk. New York: Atropos.

Virilio, Paul (2010a) *The University of Disaster*, trans. Julie Rose. Cambridge: Polity.

Virilio, Paul (2010b) *The Futurism of the Instant: Stop–Eject*, trans. Julie Rose. Cambridge: Polity.

Virilio, Paul (2012) *The Great Accelerator*, trans. Julie Rose. Cambridge: Polity.

Virilio, Paul and Armitage, John (2001) "From Modernism to Hypermodernism and Beyond," in John Armitage (ed.) *Virilio Live: Selected Interviews*. London: Sage, pp. 15–47.

Virilio, Paul and Armitage, John (2009) "In the Cities of the Beyond: An Interview with Paul Virilio," in Brigitte van der Sande (ed.) *OPEN 18: 2030: War Zone Amsterdam: Imagining the Unimaginable*. Amsterdam: NAi Publishers-SKOR, pp. 100–11.

Virilio, Paul and Armitage, John (2011) "The Third War: Cities, Conflict and Contemporary Art: Interview with Paul Virilio," in John Armitage (ed.), *Virilio Now: Current Perspectives in Virilio Studies*. Cambridge: Polity, pp. 29–45.

Virilio, Paul and Goldman, Sacha (2012) "Celebration: A World of Appearances," *Cultural Politics* 8 (1): 61–72.

Virilio, Paul and Lotringer, Sylvère (2008) *Pure War*, trans. Philip Beitchman, Brian O'Keefe, and Mark Polizzotti. New York: Semiotext(e).

Virilio, Paul and Parent, Claude (1996a) *Architecture Principe 1966 and 1996*, trans. George Collins. Besançon: Les Éditions de L'Imprimeur.

Virilio, Paul and Parent, Claude (1996b) *The Function of the Oblique*, trans. Pamela Johnson. London: Architectural Association.

Williams, Raymond (1973) *The Country and the City*. London: Chatto and Windus.

Winkel, Roel Vande and Welch, David (eds.) (2010) *Cinema and the Swastika: The International Expansion of Third Reich Cinema*. London: Palgrave.

Witcomb, Andrea (2003) *Re-Imagining the Museum: Beyond the Mausoleum*. London.

INDEX